On Freud

INSUBORDINATIONS / ITALIAN RADICAL THOUGHT
Lorenzo Chiesa, series editor

On Freud

Elvio Fachinelli

translated by Christina Chalmers
with an introduction by Gioele P. Cima

The MIT Press / Cambridge, Massachusetts / London, England

Originally published as *Su Freud*, © 2012 Adelphi Edizioni.

The translation of this work has been funded by SEPS
Segretariato Europeo per le Pubblicazioni Scientifiche

Via Val d'Aposa 7, 40123 Bologna, Italy
seps@seps.it   www.seps.it

This book was set in Arnhem Pro by Jen Jackowitz. Printed and bound in the
United States of America.

Library of Congress Cataloging-in-Publication Data

Names: Fachinelli, Elvio, author.
Title: On Freud / Elvio Fachinelli ; translated by Christina Chalmers ; introduction
    by Gioele P. Cima.
Other titles: Su Freud. English
Description: Cambridge, Massachusetts : The MIT Press, [2022] | Series:
    Insubordinations: Italian radical thought | Includes bibliographical
    references.
Identifiers: LCCN 2021046828 | ISBN 9780262047203 (hardcover)
Subjects: LCSH: Freud, Sigmund, 1856-1939. | Psychoanalysis.
Classification: LCC BF109.F74 F3313 2022 | DDC 150.19/5—dc23
LC record available at https://lccn.loc.gov/2021046828

10 9 8 7 6 5 4 3 2 1

Contents

Series Foreword

Insubordinations are creative and innovative double negations. They occur when an existing negative condition, the state of being "sub" or "under" a given order and thereby having an inferior rank, is countered by negating this very subjection. In our current late-capitalist predicament, such a reversal acquires a more complex meaning. The ordering authority is in fact no longer simply in crisis and exposed to resistance but profoundly disordered in its own operative structure. Today, powers traditionally devoted to regulation perpetuate and reinforce their effectiveness by continuously deregulating themselves. Orders become more and more oppressive precisely as they unveil the inconsistency on which they rest. As Pier Paolo Pasolini presciently put it almost fifty years ago, by now, "nothing is more anarchic than power." In this desolate scenario, actual insubordination cannot but arise as the tentative search for a *new* kind of order. Its long-term and admittedly ambitious mission is the establishment of a society without subordinates, called "communism." Its first and more realistic task is a taxonomic critique of an Order that resolves itself into myriad conflicting, yet no less tyrannical, suborders.

The present series aims to dissect the contemporary variant of the double negation involved in insubordination through the privileged prism of Italian radical thought. Starting in the late 1970s, Italy emerged as a laboratory for test-piloting the administration of the state of exception we are now living on a planetary level, both geopolitically and in our everyday lives. A brutal repression put an abrupt end to an intense season of social and political emancipations. But the theoretical elaboration of that defeat, which should not be confused with a grieving process, has managed to promote Italian radical thought to the center of a series of international debates that endeavor to define a new function and field of revolutionary politics. The series moves from the assumption that while so-called Italian Theory remains a vague and awkward category and attempts at hegemonizing it run the risk of resurrecting the idea of a national philosophy, it is beyond doubt that a growing number of left-wing Italian authors have, for good reasons, become very popular worldwide.

Drawing on philosophy, political theory, psychoanalysis, architecture, art history, anthropology, sociology, economics, and other fields, this interdisciplinary series intends to both further investigate consolidated Italian theories of emancipation and introduce authors (both present and past) who still remain largely unknown among Anglophone readers. Insubordinations: Italian Radical Thought will also foster original critical readings that pinpoint the tensions inherent to the oeu-vre of prominent progressive thinkers and develop novel dialogues with various strands of post-World War II mil-itant thought (such as heterodox Marxism, biopolitical theory, feminism of difference, social psychoanalysis, anti-psychiatry, and theories of Fascism). The series will also translate works by seminal earlier Italian authors who may be regarded as "forerunners" or critics *avant la lettre* of current trends in Italian radical thought.

It is my hope that, by delving into the titles of this series, readers will be able to appreciate the disciplined indiscipline they all share.

Lorenzo Chiesa

Elvio Fachinelli: A Dissident Psychoanalyst

1 The Life of a Dissident Psychoanalyst

Elvio Fachinelli was one of the most original and, in many respects, most controversial Italian psychoanalysts of the twentieth century. A perceptive critic, acute connoisseur, and translator of some of Freud's important works,[1] he immersed psychoanalysis into political contestation in a way few others have managed to do. It is no coincidence that in her *Storia della psicoanalisi* (History of psychoanalysis) Silvia Vegetti Finzi describes Fachinelli as one of the thinkers who were most "sensitive and responsive" to the social changes of the late twentieth century,[2] or that the French scholar Michel David considers him an unclassifiable figure, one capable of proposing a form of antiauthoritarianism of rare "sharpness and seriousness."[3]

Born in the small Alpine village of Luserna in 1928, Fachinelli spent his childhood in both Italy and France before studying medicine at the University of Pavia. He graduated with full marks and, after some hesitation, specialized in psychiatry, completed an internship at the Ospedale Maggiore in Milan, and wrote a thesis on the use of the Rorschach test in the diagnosis of obsessional neuroses. In 1962 he began his training analysis with the eminent Italian psychoanalyst Cesare Musatti,[4] at the end of which he became a member of the Società Psicoanalitica Italiana (Italian Psychoanalytic Society). In 1965, together with some leftist intellectuals,[5] Fachinelli launched the journal *Il Corpo* (The body), in which he commented on and translated such crucial psychoanalytic works as Freud's "Negation" and Wilhelm Reich's "Dialectical Materialism and Psychoanalysis." From the outset, Fachinelli regarded psychoanalytic theory and the concrete experience of everyday reality as being inextricably linked. For him, psychoanalysis was a crucial compass for understanding the social ferment of his time and, for this reason, its knowledge had to be put to the test in the context of political affiliations and tendencies. In 1967, with the rise of the student movement, he abandoned *Il Corpo* and joined the periodical *Quaderni Piacentini*, for which he penned his most important contributions on the so-called *Sessantotto Italiano*. In 1969, during the XXVI International Congress of Psychoanalysis, he organized with the Swiss psychoanalyst Berthold Rothschild a "counter-congress" to protest against the conservative drift of institutional psychoanalysis and its narrow conception of training analysis, an initiative that drew the interest of Jacques Lacan. The following year, together with leading feminists Lea Melandri and Luisa Muraro, he became a staff member of the self-managed kindergarten of Porta Ticinese in Milan, presenting the outcome of this experience first in the conference "Esperienze non autoritarie nella scuola" (Nonauthoritarian Experiences in School) and then in the book *L'erba voglio* (The grass I want).[6] With the aim of giving voice to the works and proposals of the extraparliamentary Left, *L'erba voglio* also became a journal—which Fachinelli founded and directed together with Muraro and Melandri for several years—before establishing itself as an independent publisher. In 1974, after undertaking initiatives against the authoritarianism of psychoanalysis and of the educational system, as well as attending numerous conferences on these matters, Fachinelli took part in a meeting with Lacan in Milan,[7] during which he famously refused to be appointed president of the Italian Section of the latter's school, the École Freudienne de Paris (EFP). In that same year, he collected some of his most important writings in the book *Il bambino dalle uova d'oro* (The boy with the golden eggs)[8] while continuing his work as a translator and political activist. In 1975, he recorded his political impressions of the Portuguese revolution, expressing his growing distrust of mass movements,[9] a distrust which in the following years would come to be increasingly characterized by resignation and pessimism. At the end of the 1970s, Fachinelli published *La freccia ferma* (*The Still Arrow*, 1979)[10] and engaged in the issue of drug addiction, famously polemicizing with Umberto Eco.[11] In 1983, he published what remains his most ambiguous book, *Claustrofilia*.[12] Growing increasingly distant from the revolutionary militancy of leftist politics, in 1987 he participated in the TV show *Fuori Orario* as a regular contributor on society and psychoanalysis. At that stage, he was already suffering from cancer. However, the disease did not prevent him from further lecturing at several psychoanalytic conferences, where he introduced some of the crucial themes of his last book, *La mente estatica* (The ecstatic mind, 1989).[13] Fachinelli died in Milan on December 21, 1989, and was buried in Luserna, to which he donated his rich and extensive library.

More than thirty years after his death, Fachinelli's legacy appears shrouded in an aura of perplexity. It is no exaggeration to say that, today, his thought seems sadly relegated to the margins of the history of psychoanalysis, reappearing only sporadically in the distorted form of the memorial or intellectual tribute. With some noteworthy exceptions,[14] Fachinelli has been preyed upon by what he himself scornfully defined as the "necrophagic apparatus" of the culture industry: a commemorative system based on the cyclical time of anniversaries in which knowledge is recalled as already "dead," or mourned with petty nostalgia.[15] What today seem to survive of Fachinellian psychoanalysis are mostly shreds of fragmentary concepts (ecstasy, claustrophilia, the dissidence of desire), cautiously purified of their intrinsic discomfort. Fully endorsing Fachinelli's harsh criticism of psychoanalysis would instead entail questioning the very meaning of psychoanalytic practice *tout court*. Becoming full-fledged "Fachinellians" would twist psychoanalysis (its peculiar rationalism, its epistemology of suspicion, and its adamant disproving of facts) against what it has itself become. As Fachinelli constantly reiterated over the years, psychoanalytic reason is marred by an "original sin" with which it has to perpetually reckon. Born as a practice that reveals the subject of the unconscious, psychoanalysis soon locked up its disturbing disclosure in a "sharp forest of defenses,"[16] turning into a paranoid reaction to the "threat" of the unknown. Yet, according to Fachinelli, psychoanalysis can still make a difference, as long as one continues to challenge its tendency to close in on itself, to "reabsorb and neutralize the meaning of its work."[17] Among all of the modern fields of knowledge, psychoanalysis seems to remain one of the few that still provides us with an inestimable "democratic promise,"[18] a call for equality founded not on a rigid conception of identity, but on the contingent incommensurability of each and every unconscious: a genuine politics of singularity whose unconditional unfolding can bring about profound transformations both in subjects and in late-capitalist society. Returning to Fachinelli today means putting into play this vocation to keep the unconscious "open," and thus countering the very concrete possibility that the Freudian discovery will fully be reduced to either a flat fundamentalism[19] or a trivial hedonist rant for libidinal emancipation.[20]

2 From Psychopathology to Revolutionary Psychoanalysis

Fachinelli's early writings appear to be distant from psychoanalytic theory and mainly dwell on psychiatry and psychopathology. However, they already present some discernible traits of his later thought. Each of these works aims to expand the scope of clinical knowledge and open it to a dialogue with a diverse range of theories and domains. Fachinelli's main concern as a psychiatrist specifically addresses the rejection of that parochial monism which haunts psychopathology as much as post-Freudian psychoanalysis. In this sense, what his earliest contributions set out to do was already typically Fachinellian: no statistical or scientific model can exhaust the sheer exuberance of subjectivity; clinical practice should not be expected to passively convert the patient's inner condition into the jargon of mental health, but instead translate the clinician's knowledge into concrete lived experience, into a kind of *praxis* which characterizes each subject's psychological vicissitudes as unique. For Fachinelli, both the psychiatrist and the psychoanalyst must share the same ethical motto: instead of closing themselves up in the "fortresses of knowledge," clinicians must actively *militate* in the world.

This aim is pivotal in Fachinelli's thesis in psychiatry.[21] Starting with a reassessment of the Rorschach test, he claims that obsessional neurosis is not a consistent condition, but a set of diversified and irreducible "manifestations"[22] whose components (that is, symptoms) are all equally relevant. Even if ambiguous and decidedly outdated, the Rorschach test enables the analysis of neurosis to be tied to the "fundamental structuring dimensions" of culture[23] and highlights the way that clinics and society are not merely watertight compartments, but inextricably intertwined poles. Deeming psychiatric methodology to be a mere "dictionary," a "kabbala of the human person,"[24] Fachinelli proposes to reconceptualize the Rorschach test through the lens of a phenomenological-existential perspective, so as to shift the emphasis from symptoms to the subject's diverse ways of *being in the world*.

The same intention runs through "New Meaning of Magical Design and Recovery of the Past in the Work of a Psychotic Artist,"[25] a work still indebted to psychopathology but which at the same time puts forward more far-sighted perspectives. Here, the phenomenological take on the patient's lived experience, the way in which one makes sense of one's world, remains crucial. However, the importance of psychoanalysis turns out to be more and more evident, with the unconscious acting as a fundamental speculative and theoretical referent: the "other scene" of the human psyche that endows each patient with a strong notion of subjectivity—i.e., the subject as an ineffable singularity. But it is only in 1965, with the completion of his training analysis, that Fachinelli begins to deal more thematically with psychoanalysis. That year he launches the leftist cultural journal *Il Corpo*, one of the first lay (nontechnical) journals devoted to psychoanalysis.[26] With *Il Corpo*, Fachinelli seeks to give psychoanalytic theory an overtly political dimension, scrutinizing some of the key Freudian concepts through anthropology, dialectics, and mass culture.

In his very first contribution, Fachinelli offers a translation of the hermetic Freudian text "Negation" (1925), accompanying it with an extensive critical commentary ("The Hypothesis of Destruction in Sigmund Freud")[27] in which he sharply opposes ego psychology. For Fachinelli, "Negation" constitutes a highly strategic piece of writing. Published in 1925, it would work as a watershed between the great thanatropic turning point of Freud's *Beyond the Pleasure Principle* (1920) and his more resigned *Civilization and Its Discontents* (1929), namely, between the dislodging of the Ego from its sovereign position in the psyche and the reconceptualization of the death drive as a cosmological principle.[28] According to Fachinelli, the supposed polarization between Eros and Thanatos is nothing but a *false* dualism; we are instead dealing with an asymmetrical relation in which life latches onto death as an ephemeral deviation, so that existence would figure merely as a "set of forces that resist death." In *Civilization and Its Discontents*, however, Freud took a step back, trivializing the productive tension between Eros and Thanatos into a gloomy "cosmology in which man is acted out, played by an internal Other":[29] destruction is downsized to an alien, impersonal force to be domesticated and imprisoned. It is in "Negation" that the sheer ambiguity between creation and destruction would become paramount for the structuring of the psyche. The defense mechanism of negation—that is, the emergence of an unconscious content linguistically denied—is what preserves humanity from the hoax of a "linearly continuous and optimistic" reason, that is to say, from a naïve narrative of the psyche as a smooth and seamless flow of thoughts. In other words, for Fachinelli negation reinstates the work of the negative as the most crucial component of psychoanalytic theory and practice. This is why post-Freudians have completely ignored this text: it establishes destruction and instability as the very foundation of the human psyche, endowing the psyche with the shadow of an unemployed negativity which can neither be tamed nor homologated in any way. On the other hand, negation also discloses how the most peremptory revelations of the unconscious always spring from the margins, from the most volatile and singular nuances of conscious life. Far from being coherently uniform, the psyche is always "ambiguous," "polyvalent," a machination whose functions must be deciphered not according to causal interpretations, but via "symbolic-descriptive" speculations.[30] The subject's task is to *assume* the negated truth of the unconscious as the seemingly peripheral part of discourse. Seen from the perspective of negation, psychoanalysis turns out to be an intrinsically dialectic knowledge, but with a caveat: linking psychoanalysis to dialectics does not mean reducing its basic assumptions to those of a seemingly stronger (more accurate) knowledge, but acknowledging how *both* these domains struggle with the theoretical ambiguity of the negative. Both psychoanalysis and dialectics are committed to the work of a logical sublation in which negation does not destroy but produces, does not eradicate but *creates*. If we dismiss negation, we not only neglect the death drive, but even psychoanalysis itself: "It now seems clear that the elimination of the concept of the death instinct . . . was one of the essential logical premises for the dislocation of psychoanalysis in the direction of a good socio-affective *adjustment*. By eliminating the negative . . . which always disputes desire and life, by eliminating death, it is easy to arrive at a concept of the 'ordered' and 'harmonious' progress of the personality."[31]

Fachinelli's critique of post-Freudian psychoanalysis continues in his second contribution to *Il Corpo*, "On Anal Time-Money" (1965),[32] a fierce attack on the idea that the individual develops through a rigid and prearranged "biological automatism."[33] Fachinelli rejects the term "stage," deeming it to function as a mere stopgap, an all-encompassing notion that claims to mirror human complexity as the output of a series of algorithms. Once again, it is by resorting to dialectics that Fachinelli manages to overcome post-Freudian psychoanalysis and its pitfalls: far from following an idealistic, homogeneous sequence, each psychosexual stage is a patchwork of material vicissitudes which unfold through "antithetical determinations." Since the unconscious knows no (evolutionary) linearity nor consistency, the most suitable term to describe such a twisted development is "situations":[34] specific and diverse moments in which one's libido takes on a hyperpersonal configuration and symbolism, incommensurable with that of other subjects. For Fachinelli, what he called the "anal situation" deserves particular attention, as its dynamics reflect not only the way in which the unconscious shapes and organizes its contents into symbolic representations, but also the primordial structuring of temporality itself. In the anal situation, we can see how time stems from a material integration of imaginary formations and symbols, affecting the mind with its composite and nested architecture. Subjective time is nothing but a "broken history," a nonlinear network of "antithesis" and "antagonistic elements."[35]

In his third contribution to *Il Corpo*, Fachinelli translates and comments on Wilhelm Reich's "Dialectical Materialism and Psychoanalysis," repudiating Reich's materialistic approach to the unconscious and instead emphasizing the importance of a multidisciplinary framework for psychoanalysis. The text also anticipates in some ways Fachinelli's dissatisfaction with communism's inability to account for abrupt political changes as well as his own need to venture into new initiatives. In 1967, he joins *Quaderni Piacentini*, published by a left-wing group strongly opposed to both mass ideology and neocapitalist optimism.[36] During these months, Fachinelli publishes some of his most important texts and brings together many of his previous arguments from what he himself defines as a "bio-psycho-sociological" perspective. In "Dissident Desire" (1968), probably his best-known yet controversial essay, Fachinelli welcomes the rise of the youth movement as a veritable political event—an absolute novelty alien both to orthodox Italian Marxism and to psychoanalysis.[37] While the movement did not give voice to the needs of any particular social class—if anything, its unusual militancy aimed to overcome social class itself and gathered together people from each and every strata of society—its non-conceptual dissidence broke with the model of Oedipal transgression postulated by Freudian psychoanalysis. According to Fachinelli, the desire which enlivened the movement was a matter of neither class consciousness nor the satisfaction of needs, but a newborn utopian-maniacal drive fundamentally incompatible with modern industrial societies.

As Fachinelli puts it, for a long time the "politics of needs" guaranteed the preservation of the status quo by providing a veritable "area of collusion" between the conservative and revolutionary sides of politics. In other words, parliamentary parties worked together to create the need for a new "reality principle," passing off a sneaky "call to order" as an "absolute" claim about "reality."[38] This covert complicity led to an inability to conceptualize the excess of desire and its absolute dissipative force. Moreover, even psychoanalysis proved to be thoroughly deaf to the movement's demands, stubbornly taking the 1968 events as yet another form of opposition to paternal authority. But dissent from the father, Fachinelli counters, has nothing to do with the young revolutionaries' requests. Quite the contrary, the figure of the father at stake here is "faded," utterly indifferent to "the situations of conflict . . . classically described by Freud." Paternal authoritarianism gives way to an "unconditional" and "total" relationship, to a more subtle and basic type of power which Freudian analysis itself "had barely glimpsed."[39] In other words, what these young revolutionaries rebelled against was the suffocating constraints of the new industrial society, a new form of control embodied in a deadly relationship with a mother who is at the same time both satiating (i.e., placing no limits on the satisfaction of needs) and devouring (i.e., strangling subjectivity at its roots). In this regard, Fachinelli identifies two key aspects that distinguish the youth movement from ordinary forms of insubordination: a request for the "impossible," for something that is outside the repressive code of needs; and the "anonymity" of the insurgents, that is, their foreignness to class structure, their fluid, immanent "equal[ity]."[40] The merging of these two aspects underlines that what is crucial is not so much the "object" of desire but its "state": the utter immanence of desire as an obstinate and "perennial NOT ENOUGH":[41] an objectless absolute thrust which plays against any conceivable form of compromise.

3 Communalization and Sectarianization: Beyond the Logic of Desire

While Fachinelli was initially fascinated by the youth protests, the publication of "Closed Group or Open Group?"[42] (1968) marks a drastic reduction of his revolutionary enthusiasm. Less than a year after the events of 1968, dissidence has come to a standstill and its praised novelty seems already integrated into the social fabric. Instead of dismantling society and institutions, the vibrant logic of desire did nothing but bring to light "a general lack of meaning," "a great void" that the "old organizational forms" soon managed to compensate for.[43] The nomadic spreading of desire was captured by leaders and members of parliament, precipitating the movement into the same (reactionary) deadlocks of mainstream politics and reformist principles.

Despite the deliberate step back from "Dissident Desire," "Closed Group or Open Group?" remains crucial to understanding Fachinelli's political militancy in those years. Instead of imparting a theoretical lesson, Fachinelli prefers to set up a concrete group analysis in which the repression, authoritarianism, and exclusion glimpsed in the revolutionary movement could be experienced directly. Relying on a broad notion of "otherness" (in which the Other represents the new, the different, but also the stranger), Fachinelli addresses the students' intrinsic tendency to transform the Other into an enemy, namely, into a *threat* which has to be kept at bay or even abruptly excluded: "The extraneous, the concrete, and tangible (all too tangible) that is dissimilar had to be eliminated . . . to make room for an ever more perfect *sameness*."[44] To grasp the purging processes inherent to the group, Fachinelli proposes a logical scheme that Massimo Recalcati has appropriately defined as the "antinomian pair of opening-closing," a device that in his subsequent works Fachinelli develops in different guises, and that according to Recalcati would have "the same dignity [that] the categories of Eros and Thanatos have in Freud, those of desire and enjoyment in Lacan, and those of molar and molecular in Deleuze and Guattari."[45] In "Closed Group or Open Group?," polarization unfolds through the processes of what Fachinelli calls

"communalization [*accomunamento*]" and "sectarianization [*settarizzazione*]." As Fachinelli remarks, we should
resist the temptation to see them as a mere dichotomy.
On the contrary, communalization and sectarianization
are entangled in a complex intersection, in which they
continuously merge with one another. Whereas communalization prompts an unhesitant acceptance of otherness, enhancing the human tendency to aggregate and
communicate with the Other, sectarianization marks a
reaction that tightens the group's borders, closing them
against a threatening and hostile outside. Yet, instead
of preserving the group identity, this paranoid closure
ends up exposing it to the risk of its own implosion and
collapse. Therefore, when sectarianization seems to
prevail and the group begins to crumble, there may be
a return to communalization, a desperate reopening to
the outside. The failure of the revolutionary movement
consisted precisely in its having succumbed to closure,
ossifying its exuberance in the figure of the leader, who
absorbed the heterogeneity of the group's desires. In
order to establish a solid identity among its members,
sectarianization fosters the homogenization of the
group and enables the leader to control its members in
a unitary and authoritative way. The weaker the group is,
the more it will tend to lock onto itself, and therefore to
become "persecutory," "fragmented," and unstable. At
this point, there are two possible outcomes: either a renewed communalization, or devitalization. Nonetheless,

Fachinelli is forced to conclude that, most of the time, sectarianization prevails over communalization, thus dooming the group to its self-annihilation: every revolution that struggles for equality and freedom inevitably fails, crushed under its own tendency to closure and the need to expel what resists it.

Post-1968 disillusionment allows Fachinelli to intensify his reflection on the sectarian nature of groups. In July 1969, this leads to his organization, with Berthold Rothschild, of a "counter-congress" to protest against the 26th IPA Congress in Rome. The purpose of the initiative is once again to challenge the psychoanalytic establishment, an objective that Fachinelli subsequently pursues in his pivotal intervention "What Does Oedipus Ask the Sphinx?" (1969),[46] in which he introduces his famous dichotomy between a "psychoanalysis of questions" and a "psychoanalysis of answers." Today, Fachinelli writes, psychoanalysis is no longer a practice of questions, a knowledge which interrogates the subject about his or her symptoms, but an authority which merely *prescribes* answers: "Psychoanalysis . . . has increasingly deteriorated into . . . the task of giving reasons to what exists, that is, to rationalize its irrationalities, prevent its difficulties, buffer its conflicts."[47]

In sharp contrast to Freud's teaching, Oedipus's encounter with the Sphinx has lost its initiatory value as a challenge through which man assumes his destiny—that is, the truth of his symptom. Completely misunderstanding its original vocation, psychoanalysis has taken the position of a despotic Sphinx, "the stranger who waits for the traveler to come along" in order to impose on him answers of unquestionable and universal value.[48] The subversive singularity of the symptom is thus reduced to procedures of "serial indoctrination," employed by what Fachinelli calls "the official fortresses of knowledge"—and psychoanalysis itself, suffocated by a massive bureaucracy, becomes in every respect an *accomplice* in the "control of deviance."

However, such an institutional fortification does not seal the triumph of psychoanalytic knowledge, its ultimate universalization, but instead ends up revealing its "serious conceptual crisis."[49] Once again, sectarianization as a closing reflex reveals the group's inherent weakness, its desperate attempt to resist dissolution by closing onto itself. Faced with the novelty of the youth movement and its "impossible" demands, psychoanalysis was unable to renew its conceptual apparatus, to offer people a new language to grasp the world's dynamic changes: what does the old oedipal paternalism still have to say to the new "children" of late capitalism? Fachinelli's diagnosis is equally ruthless and clear: psychoanalysis has failed, but this does not mean that we should also reject the psychoanalytic method as such. Instead, psychoanalysis needs to be reconstructed in "other places," outside the logic of ego psychology and its institutional borders. What we desperately need is a psychoanalysis of the "irregular," of the "arrhythmic," a "labor with no fixed abode" which, instead of trying to rationalize what already exists, is committed to the enhancement of human contingency.[50]

4 After the Revolution: The Endless Labor of Psychoanalysis

During the 1970s, Fachinelli's urge to formulate a new psychoanalytic language from the lower steps of the social ladder takes shape through a close dialogue with the discontent to be found on the fringes of society—working-class and inner-city districts, public schools. Nonetheless, such a political impetus is also ceaselessly accompanied by an animated commitment to theoretical reelaboration. Although he was disheartened by the failed revolution, the Fachinelli of the 1970s does not hesitate to engage in the most controversial and delicate issues of late-capitalist society, such as the problems of education, drug addiction, and social exclusion.

At the very beginning of the decade, together with Melandri (who would later also become his partner) and Muraro, Fachinelli joins the staff of the self-managed kindergarten of Porta Ticinese in Milan. Fachinelli's militancy about school and education reforms began as early as 1967, with his clear opposition to the primitiveness of the mainstream educational model. In a late interview, he admits that it was Don Lorenzo Milani's

Lettera a una professoressa (Letter to a teacher), a book that exposed the impact of social class dynamics on the school system, that triggered his interest in the events of 1968. In his review of the volume, Fachinelli emphasizes the selective and exclusionary nature of Italian education, identifying it with the very "root of our impotent segregation."[51] According to Fachinelli and Milani, culture in the school system functions as a highly separatist and disguised "moral screen," which needs to be replaced by a new system "that does not fail [pupils], which lasts three hundred and sixty-five days a year," and which is based on an idea of "endless training."[52] Two years later, Fachinelli revisits the topic of education in his translation of and commentary on Walter Benjamin's "Program for a Proletarian Children's Theater" (1969),[53] highlighting the importance of a proletarian (democratic, noncoercive, and egalitarian) education and opposing it to the bourgeois (classist) one. Written before his participation in the Porta Ticinese kindergarten experience, this contribution already argues for a type of education based not on such bourgeois values as meritocracy and coercion, but on improvisation and representation, an education that guarantees children "the fulfilment of their childhood." In line with Benjamin's thesis, Fachinelli views children's expressive freedom to be purely "revolutionary"[54] insofar as it is impervious to subtle class ideologies. Broadly speaking, there are two main reasons why education is such a crucial issue for Fachinelli. First, given that education addresses a personality which is still developing (and thus not yet alienated by the standardizing logic of consumerism), it is part and parcel of our responsibility for the future.[55] Second, Fachinelli's take on education also enables him to rework his postrevolutionary viewpoint on psychoanalysis. In that same year, in the programmatic paper "The Psychoanalyst Must Define His Position in Society" (1970), he proposes that psychoanalysis is amenable to "more social" tasks, but only under one fundamental condition: to offer psychoanalysis to anyone who needs it requires the fabrication of new explanatory models, the elaboration of new concepts to cope with "different requests."[56] Since human concerns are closely intertwined with those of the community, psychoanalysis must overcome its obsolete bourgeois segregation and become comprehensible to everyone. In this sense, the self-managed kindergarten experience is not an impromptu initiative, but the practical application of diverse ideas about the importance of acting within and in favor of school education. Although short-lived, this experiment continued in the conference Non-Authoritarian Experiences in School, whose proceedings were published as *L'erba voglio* (The grass I want).

And it is precisely in the homonymous journal *L'erba voglio* that Fachinelli pens one of his most famous theoretical texts, "The Paradox of Repetition,"[57] a long article published in three parts between 1971 and 1973. The basic objective of the paper is to criticize the Freudian compulsion to repeat, splitting its univocal model into three different modes of repetition. Fachinelli's return to an eminently theoretical discussion of psychoanalysis is anything but random: after the kindergarten initiative, he acknowledges that psychoanalysis alone is capable of providing society with a truly emancipatory anthropological basis for the individual, a unique knowledge that enhances subjectivity without dissipating it in the capitalist tide of consumerism or in the collectivization of the Marxist theory of class struggle.

Fachinelli argues that Freud limited himself to showing only the "bad side" of repetition, conceiving it as a forced, rigidly deterministic, and unilateral mechanism. Freudian repetition freezes time in an eternal and unchangeable reiteration of the past, which leaves no room for the subject to be responsible for and act upon his own future. Moreover, Fachinelli notes that if there is no possibility to change the future, if one is inexorably consigned to repetition, then the present itself also turns into yet another past: "For Freud . . . the past becomes the present: it is transference, acting out. . . . But in this way, the present almost does not exist for itself, it does not have an effect; and since past experience turns out to be, in large part, 'beyond the pleasure principle,' its repetition tends to be a repetition of the negative."[58] Such a vision of the present is problematic not only in that it simplifies the concrete complexity of human experience, but also because of its (narrow) political outcomes: to say that man's future will inexorably be a copy of the past is to deprive the subject of any ability to choose and foster (social) change. Fachinelli instead proposes an account of repetition built on three different variants. The first mode of repetition is the replica, "an almost precise reedition of the already given," which passively superimposes the past onto the present. The second type is reduction, an impoverished and "more schematic" repetition. Finally, there is resumption (*ripresa*), a repetition that, while catalyzing the reappearance of the past, puts life back into action, opening it to confirmation or modification. Fachinelli remarks that "repetition is only a general term," which indicates "various possibilities" and "distinct modalities."[59] Unlike the monotony or simplification that go with repetition in the first two senses of the term, resumption allows us to *reactualize* the past, opening it to change and transformation. Moreover, since reality is complex, asymmetrical, riddled with unbridgeable disparities, the past is always irreversible: we will never be able to flawlessly reproduce it. Fachinelli opposes the idea of an unethical subject, chained to the inertia of the past that repeats itself indefinitely and inexorably, and instead offers a notion of nonnegative repetition, which exacerbates the urgency to take a stand for our own unconscious subjectivity, and therefore revitalize our choices. Most importantly, such a discourse not only concerns the clinic but can also be extended to the very structure of the psychoanalytic establishment. As Fachinelli argues in a polemic with Giovanni Jervis, it will not be the reactionary repetition of the affiliation mechanisms of power (that is, training analysis) that rescues psychoanalysis from its decline, but psychoanalysis's resumption: in a world in constant transformation, psychoanalysis will survive not by resisting sociopolitical mutations, but by placing itself in the position of those who know how to ask the right questions. Relinquishing its status as a restricted institution of repetition, psychoanalysis must instead present itself as the voice of resumption.[60]

5 The Question of Time

The question of time at stake in the notion of resumption becomes even more crucial in Fachinelli's subsequent works. We could even say that his reflections on temporality mark his most original contribution to psychoanalysis. What is time? And what is its relationship with the unconscious? Is it enough to claim, as Freud did, that the unconscious is timeless? All of these questions converge in *The Still Arrow: Three Attempts to Annul Time* (1979), a book in which Fachinelli aims to integrate Freud's legacy with some of his own personal accounts of the theory and practice of psychoanalysis. While Fachinelli previously tried to update and enhance Freud's hypotheses, in *The Still Arrow* he reverses his approach:

it no longer remains faithful to Freud, but instead emphasizes and works through the very conditions that make psychoanalysis equally prominent and problematic. For this to be possible, however, we must undertake new modes of expression and fabricate a new language external to that of ordinary metapsychology. As Fachinelli puts it in the opening of the book, *The Still Arrow* is "almost entirely devoid of psychoanalytic terminology": "Not only because the latter has become entrenched in hypostatised formulas—in both specialised and common use—that often hinder, instead of facilitating, the understanding of concrete situations; but especially because, following the thread of discovery, I was obliged to go beyond the psychoanalytic field and deal also with other problems, which are formulated differently."[61]

The key notion Fachinelli introduces here, which links the three studies proposed by the book into one substantial argument, is that of the *chronotype*: the singular way in which the subject, a society, or any other group shapes their own personal experience with time. The chronotype is an "element that orders . . . events" and "situations . . . [which are] completely disconnected";[62] it is a theoretical device that, rather than claiming to solve the problem of time, exacerbates it. Time is a concern that haunted Fachinelli's thought since his youth, but it is only in *The Still Arrow* that it emerges as a central matter for "the future of psychoanalysis and its interventions."[63] As the book's subtitle states, this study aims to analyze the way in which certain clinical, anthropological, and sociohistorical structures deal with time, attempt to dominate it, and therefore annul it. Obsessive-compulsive rituals, archaic societies, and Fascism would equally be captured by the same chronotype, in which time is manipulated and subsequently denied. With regard to the obsessive, this kind of subject carries out a molecular "segmentation of concrete time" into a "series of timelets (*tempuscoli*),"[64] each separated from the other. By annulling time, that is, by splitting it into infinite micro-times, the obsessive can indefinitely postpone the completion of the action that distresses him most. This "'stationary' condition" of "permanent restlessness"[65] would then unfold in a network of interpersonal relationships and desires, giving way to a veritable "archaic micro-society."[66] Accordingly, for Fachinelli, Fascism emerges from the "denial of the death of the fatherland"—from the unacceptable collapse of nationalist ideals following World War I. This is why Fascism opposed the idea of a "trampled," "damaged" nation with a "total," statuesque, and immobile but also "exclusive and intolerant" fatherland, which punished in its "opponents . . . [its] own fantasies about killing the [fatherland]."[67] To disguise the "irremediable disappearance" of a lost national unity, Fascism had to endlessly reenact its phantom of a total communion, encapsulating it in an infinite "time of return."[68] Fascism and obsessional neurosis in turn significantly resonate with the rites of archaic societies. According to the basic assumption of such societies that "the dead man is not dead" but "keeps on living" through his celebration in rites, the fear of the corpse as something dragged out of time leads their members to the denial of "death itself."[69] The archaic chronotype is one of sheer *plenitude*, in which the negativity of death is constantly reinstated as a living social and spiritual entity.

The gist of the chronotype is therefore clear: the anguish of time is a primordial phenomenon which has always accompanied human affairs, and its understanding does not rely on some particular or even scientific objectification. Rather, time can be approached only through an inquiry into how each subject or social institution acts on (and is acted upon by) it.

In the early 1980s, Fachinelli positions temporality at the heart of psychoanalytic practice itself. His book *Claustrofilia* (1983) explores the nature of analytic time, a *terra incognita* that not even Freud was able to explore. Psychoanalytic knowledge was never questioned in terms of its own uncertainty and moments of bewilderment. Both the chronotype and the claustrophilic space pinpoint the same heterogeneous compression of several temporal phenomena and situations, but unlike the chronotype, claustrophilia addresses an even more intimate, unfathomable time, which comprises dreams, "birth-childbirth fantasies," "pregnancy-uterine states," and the "primal scene."[70] What all of these situations have in common is a basic "search for closure," a propensity for "locking oneself in."[71] Even though Fachinelli's attempt to track down this primordial tendency in a range of other experiences (such as *Doppelgänger* phenomena or certain unconscious coincidences) is not always convincing, the importance of claustrophilia to psychoanalysis is paramount in that it brings to light one of its most controversial issues: *the length of the psychoanalytic treatment*. As Fachinelli argues, the claustrophilic area plays a "hidden" but nonetheless "active" role in the analytic relationship, to such an extent that without this notion psychoanalysis would not even be conceivable. Criticizing Freud, Fachinelli claims that between the (patently experimental) *Studies on Hysteria* and the subsequent (and methodologically defined) *Technical Papers* the notion of analytic time underwent a significant reworking: while in its first formulation, temporality was still "semifeudal," "discontinuous," and punctuated by the emergence of unconscious symptoms, its subsequent conception became "chronometric" and "monotonous." Once the analytical method was standardized, "the implicit values of regularity and continuity . . . come to occupy first place in opposition to those of transformation and change," bringing about a paradoxical result: while the length of individual psychoanalytic sessions is reduced to a mere social convention (a defined time, purged of its wasted and empty moments), the total duration of the treatment becomes "indefinite," immersed in an interminable time without visible limits.[72] The transition of psychoanalysis from an exploratory practice of the unconscious to a normalizing institution follows exactly the development of this relationship, and the analyst is no longer devoted to the search for unexpected variations, but now seeks *the preservation of a regularity*. Like a "maternal omnivorous figure,"[73] the analyst exploits the analysand's claustrophilic space (his primordial desire to "lock himself in") to turn analysis into an endless treatment. This is why Fachinelli sardonically concludes that the psychoanalytic apparatus has come to a "standstill," that it itself has become yet another attempt to annul time.

Fachinelli's speculation on temporality reaches its apex in his final book, *La mente estatica* (The ecstatic mind, 1989), which sets forth a new reading of the concept of ecstasy. Fachinelli's notion of the ecstatic is remarkably broad, in that he repudiates the use of a unitary conception of ecstasy and denies its immediate traceability to a specific cognitive or emotional state. Rather than something clearly delimited, the ecstatic is "a border area," the extreme and at the same time most intimate margin of human experience.[74] In this sense, Fachinelli's ecstasy has nothing to do with the possession states famously described by anthropologists, or with the clinical stigma of dissociation, and for one fundamental reason: Fachinelli completely rejects the idea that subjectivity might be falsified or somehow "squeezed" out of the body. In ecstasy, the subject does not dissolve, but *expands*, while on the contrary it is the Ego that is abolished: by suspending the "vigilance-defense system," subjectivity is invested with an "unusual . . . excessive . . . joy," which leads it beyond itself.[75] And it is precisely the relationship between ecstasy and temporality that allows for such a joyful expansion: rather than putting time out of joint, ecstasy takes the individual out of time, creating a fissure in the temporal frame whereby subjectivity detaches itself from identity and thrives in an unlimited multiplicity: "At certain points, something, anything, is timeless, and I watch it exist. But I am only a gaze of the thing that is, its way of being in the light."[76]

Although apparently foreign to psychoanalysis, ecstatic subjectivity turns out to be its most critical reversal, a fundamental reference to undermine from within what Fachinelli defines as the "apologies of defense," namely, those discourses that propose an account of the individual as perennially vulnerable, constantly besieged by a need to defend himself or herself. Since its destiny runs parallel to the mass popularization of psychoanalysis, ecstasy is not only a fascinating theoretical notion, but first and foremost something genuinely political. The apology of defense as the discourse which represses the ecstatic in fact emerged together with psychoanalysis, as its side effect, and silently spread with its institutionalization, to the point of triggering a *total medicalization* of Western society. According to Fachinelli, Freud himself noted the danger of the ecstatic (which is its ability to disintegrate reason), and consequently he confined it to a domain of paroxysmal but unpleasant experience. Menaced by a "boundless joy," psychoanalysis walled off the ecstatic and progressively slipped into a discourse that, instead of giving voice to the unconscious, reduced it to "the size of the barriers built against it."[77] When joy manifests itself uncontrollably, the defense "snaps like a trap," entangling the subject in a state of paranoid vigilance.[78] The logical primacy of defenses ends up producing a deadly short circuit within psychoanalytic knowledge, extending the defensive attitude of the unconscious to the sphere of the ordinary, and therefore of the nonpathological. Psychoanalytic defensive mechanisms (and this is even more valid for current psychotherapy)[79] acquire a normative value with respect to the individual's entire psychic life, establishing a problematic continuity between the state of alteration (so-called pathology) and that of nonalteration, which makes civilization as a whole something intrinsically pathological. Fachinelli's conclusion is clear and resigned: instead of setting subjectivity free from the constraints of capitalist reason, psychoanalysis has renewed and reinforced these constraints, thus completely disregarding its original vocation.

6 *On Freud*, or, On the Fate of Psychoanalysis

What position does *On Freud*—a short posthumous book—occupy in Elvio Fachinelli's thought? And what could it tell us about the puzzling conclusions of *The Ecstatic Mind*? In a sense, we might say that it is *transversal* to the whole of Fachinelli's work. The essays in this collection are a very precious thread for clarifying, singling out, and even reelaborating some of the most delicate aspects of Fachinelli's critique of consumer society and, above all, of psychoanalysis itself. The volume collects six texts, of which the first, "Freud," dates back to 1966, at the beginning of Fachinelli's psychoanalytic militancy, while the last, "The Unexpected and Surprise in Analysis," was written in 1989, just prior to his death. Despite its brevity, the collection is extremely heterogeneous and faithfully mirrors the intense activity carried out on several fronts by its author. "Freud," for example—an entry originally written for one of the volumes of the series *The Protagonists of Universal History*—is striking for its ability to weave the theoretical foundations of psychoanalysis together with a surprising number of personal observations and findings about Freud the person. Rather than proceeding through an aseptic introduction to the father of psychoanalysis, Fachinelli adopts instead a series of parallax perspectives: Freud the conquistador, who leads psychoanalysis to the exploration of new fields of knowledge; Freud the archaeologist, who discovers antithetical and incongruous elements in the territory of the unconscious; but also Freud the Victorian, whose bourgeois values clashed with the revolutionary character of his discovery. Fachinelli's line of thought is unambiguous. If the truth of psychoanalysis is a truth of "labor," that is, of the active confrontation with contradiction, then this concerns not only the unconscious, but the very stability of the analytical method itself—what Fachinelli describes as "the core of the psychoanalytic method": the tendency of the Freudian discovery to constantly navigate between the confirmation/repetition and the refutation/falsification of its own foundations, between the preservation of the past and the inscrutability of the future.

This is why *On Freud*'s main thesis is as strong as it is problematic: psychoanalysis can only be the most ambiguous and fragile form of knowledge, a sensational discovery that oscillates all too easily between a "disturbing grandeur" and a reactionary "flatness," between an epistemologically uncertain and alien body of research and a discipline "'preyed upon' culturally" by power and modern forms of control. Freud's uncertainties over how to transmit his discovery are the same uncertainties psychoanalysis must confront today, and they can be summarized in what, in his last intervention, Fachinelli considers to be "the analytic *epoché*": by barricading itself within its own knowledge, by adjusting its main concepts to a mechanical administration of the unconscious, psychoanalysis has lost its "light-ness." In the analytic experience, there seems to be no more room for the unexpected, the wager, and surprise. Indeed, the entire device proceeds by repetition of the "already known," constantly marred by the fear of those moments in which it enters into a crisis and is threat-ened by the breaking-in of the "unexpected."

Fachinelli's remarkable critical ability consists of ex-tending this psychoanalytic securitarian tendency to a set of surprisingly variable situations. In the last period of his work, he detects this reflex to close in on itself not only in the transmission of analytic knowledge (namely, training analysis and its conceptual apparatus) but also at the heart of the analytic relationship. It is no coinci-dence, Fachinelli writes, that the most compromising of these situations has historically been embodied in the capitalist symptom of the "phobia of the gift," that is, in psychoanalysis's inability (from Freud to today) to disregard its "money economy": "Every historical mo-ment, individual or collective, in which the money rela-tionship, the mercenary relationship, reveals its limits and is exceeded, even fleetingly, is also a moment when the institutional analytic relationship enters into crisis."

Curiously, while the analysand is expected to tell "the most secret details of his perversions," the analyst is si-lent about "*his*" money,[80] treating it as an unquestionable aspect of the psychoanalytic setting. Therefore, while *The Ecstatic Mind* seemed to evoke a vague nostalgia for

a sort of lost analytical purity, for an inquiry into the unconscious prior to closure and self-defense discourses,
the writings of *On Freud* produce a formidable change
of perspective, speculating that although post-Freudian
psychoanalysis degenerated into a gigantic misunderstanding, the most sinful of these moments is to be
found in Freud himself. In other words, the medicalizing
degeneration of the unconscious—the "sharp forest of
defenses" that psychoanalysis has erected against it—is
no longer to be read against the background of Freud's
heirs, but as the other side of the birth of psychoanalysis
tout court. Freud's inability to accept the "gift"—namely,
to experience the "vital, free, liberating" joy of gratitude
without resorting to a "disturbing central instance of
authority"—would constitute for Fachinelli the incho-
ate *destiny* of analytic decay. And it is precisely in this
interstice between Freud's original sin and capitalist society that Fachinelli outlines what is probably his most
audacious reflection, namely, the distinction between a
mass psychoanalysis and a democratic psychoanalysis,
between psychoanalysis as a practice of standardization
and social control and a psychoanalysis of singularity.
For Fachinelli, as long as psychoanalysis remains caught
in the "straitjacket of exchange," it will not be able to
evade its bourgeois trap, its structural exclusion of the
poorest sections of the population. But opening psychoanalysis to everyone (i.e., to the masses), spreading it
throughout the world without compromising it, would

still mean standardizing its knowledge, transforming it into yet another instrument of homologation or, as Fachinelli has it, a "huge zombie."[81] Psychoanalysis cannot become a universal praxis for everyone if it does not elaborate its bond to money as a choice that is no longer (and never has been) "obligatory."

Although Fachinelli does not unfold this point any further, his proposal is more urgent than ever if the future scope and responsibilities of the psychoanalytic intervention are to be established. In a world in which psychotherapeutic culture has now colonized much of the Western imaginary and terminology, Fachinelli's work remains extremely topical and allows us to engage with the possibility of a new and less authoritarian path to the disturbing knowledge of the unconscious—a democratic practice in which the free "encounter" with the singularity of the Sphinx becomes close to "what the Greeks called good or bad fortune, *tyche*," while preserving a constant dialogue with *ananke*, that is, with "the inevitability of the destiny of all of us."

Gioele P. Cima

On Freud

Freud

1856 Sigmund is born on May 6, in Freiberg, now Příbor (Moravia), the first child of the marriage of Jacob Freud—a Jewish fabrics trader—and Amalia Nathansohn. His father already has two children, born of a previous marriage.

1860 As a consequence of the economic crisis, worsening after the Austro-Italian war of 1859, Jacob Freud, semi-ruined, moves permanently to Vienna. Sigmund's two half-brothers emigrate instead to Manchester, England.

1865–1872 A year earlier than is normal, Sigmund enters the Sperl Gymnasium. In his scholastic career he is first in the class. In 1872 he brilliantly passes his graduation exams and decides to become a doctor, giving up the idea of studying law, after hearing a reading of the essay "Nature," attributed to Goethe. A crash in the stock market in Vienna causes Jacob Freud to lose his capital. The family is forced to turn to Amalia's relatives for help.

1876 Sigmund's first researches in comparative anatomy (confirming the existence of testicles in male eel). In October he enters the Institute of Physiology directed by Professor Ernst Brücke. Here he meets Joseph Breuer.

1877–1882 Research on the histology of the nervous system in Brücke's laboratory.

1881 Doctor of Medicine. From now on, he will be almost independent of his family, and will be given help by his friends in the medical profession, particularly by Breuer.

1882 In April, he meets Martha Bernays, with whom he becomes secretly engaged in June. After a conversation with Brücke from which he gets confirmation that he has no prospects at the Institute of Physiology, he decides to give up pure research and devote himself to practical medicine. At the end of July he starts to visit the wards of Vienna's general hospital.

1883 Breuer informs Freud about the case of Anna O., a hysteric he had begun to treat with the "cathartic method" in 1880. Freud works in the brain anatomy laboratory of the psychiatric clinic directed by Professor Meynert.

1884 He publishes "The Structure of the Elements of the Nervous System,"[82] in which he claims, on the basis of his research in Brücke's laboratory, the morphological and physiological unity of nerve cells and fibers, thus prefiguring Waldeyer's theory of the neuron (1891). He begins to study the pharmacological properties of cocaine, which he notes has an energetic antidepressant effect on himself. He predicts the anesthetic action of this alkaloid and suggests to his friend Königstein that he test it on ocular diseases. It is a colleague of his, Koller, who a few months later begins to "revolutionize eye surgery with the use of cocaine." A close friend from Freud's time with Brücke, Ernst von Fleischl, abuses the new drug, thinking he is weaning himself off morphine, and suffers severe drug poisoning.

1885 First attempts at hypnotic treatment. In January he submits his academic curriculum vitae—"the first sketch of my biography"—to obtain the title of *Privatdozent* in neuropathology, which will be granted to him on September 5. In June he wins a scholarship for graduates, which allows him to go to a foreign institute for six months. On October 13 he begins attending the ward of Charcot, the most illustrious neurologist of his time, at the Salpêtrière hospital in Paris. While continuing his studies in the histology of the nervous system, he is little by little attracted to psychopathology through his interest in Charcot's conception of hysteria. From this moment on, he will become a pure clinician.

1886 In early April he returns to Vienna; on the 25th he opens a private clinic, which will provide him only very modest earnings over a long period. On September 13 he marries Martha Bernays, with whom he will have six children. In October he presents a case of male hysteria with hemi-anesthesia to the Vienna Society of Medicine: he gets a cold reception, especially from his teacher Meynert, who gradually excludes him from his laboratory. Freud's private clientele is made up almost exclusively of neurotics, whom he treats with electrotherapy, but he soon realizes that the effect is of a suggestive nature. Reports of cocaine mania increase around the world, and Freud is accused by Erlenmeyer of having introduced "the third scourge of mankind."

1887 In November he meets Wilhelm Fliess, a Berlin otolaryngologist, with whom he begins a correspondence that will last until 1902. He abandons electrotherapy for hypnotic suggestion. Neurological publications.

1888 Comparative study of organic and hysterical paralyses. He encounters various difficulties in the hypnotic treatment of his patients.

1889 With Mrs. Emmy von N., he applies Breuer's cathartic method for the first time. In July, he stays in Nancy, with Liébault and Bernheim, to perfect his hypnotic technique.

1891 He publishes *On Aphasia*,[83] dedicated to Breuer, in which he criticizes the classical theory of aphasia, inspired by the functional approach of John Hughlings Jackson. The family moves to Berggasse 19, where Freud will live until 1938.

1892 Together with Breuer, he writes "On the Psychical Mechanism of Hysterical Phenomena: Preliminary Communication" [*SE*, 2: 3–17]. In it he argues that the cause of hysteria is not psychic trauma, as Charcot thought, but its memory, which has been repressed. "Hysterics suffer primarily from reminiscences." In "A Case of Successful Treatment by Hypnotism" [*SE*, 1: 115–130], he argues that the origin of neurotic symptoms lies in the existence of ideas antithetical to conscious ones and of an unconscious counter-will.

1895 He collects the work of previous years in *Studies on Hysteria* [*SE*, 2], written together with Breuer, who however refuses to follow him in the conception of the sexual origin of neuroses. This is the end of their collaboration. Faced with growing anti-Semitism, he joins the B'nai B'rith Jewish Masonic lodge.

1896 In an article for the *Revue Neurologique*, Freud uses the term "psychoanalysis" for the first time. After a glacial reception of one of his communications on the sexual etiology of hysteria at the Vienna Society for Psychiatry and Neurology, he decides not to attend medical gatherings anymore. On October 23 his father dies.

1897 Freud publishes his last work on neurology. In May he decides to write a book on dreams, which he had begun to analyze in 1894. In July he begins a systematic self-analysis. On October 15, he announces to Fliess his discovery of the Oedipus complex.

1898 First open disagreements with Fliess.

1899 *The Interpretation of Dreams* is concluded [*SE*, 4–5], which appears, with the date 1900, in November 1899. The book receives almost no reception in scientific circles.

1900 In August, last meeting with Fliess.

1901 Trip to Rome with his brother Alexander. He wrote of it as "the crucial point of my life," the first of the seven visits he will make to this city. A doctor who attended his university lectures, Max Kahane, talks to Wilhelm Stekel about the new treatment method. Stekel, suffering from a neurotic disturbance, begins an analytic treatment with Freud.

1902 At the suggestion of a colleague who has "personally experienced the benefits of analytic therapy"—probably Stekel—Freud begins to gather his few friends and followers regularly in the waiting room of his office, once a week. It is the "Wednesday Psychological Society," of whose debates Stekel gives an account in the Sunday edition of the *Neues Wiener Tagblatt*.

1904 Freud publishes *The Psychopathology of Everyday Life* [*SE*, 6], which had been published in periodical form three years earlier. In Athens, while on the Acropolis he has an unusual psychological experience, which he analyzes, thirty-two years later, in a letter to Romain Rolland. He learns of the interest in psychoanalysis emerging at Burghölzli, the famous Zurich psychiatric clinic directed by Eugen Bleuler, inspired by his chief assistant Carl Gustav Jung. In 1906 a regular correspondence between Freud and Jung begins.

1907–1910 *Delusions and Dreams in Jensen's "Gradiva"* [*SE*, 9: 3–95], the first published example of the application of the psychoanalytic method to a fictional work. Visits to Freud begin: Jung, Binswanger, Abraham (1907); Ferenczi, Jones (1908); Pfister (1909); and Sachs (1910), as the first foreign psychoanalytic societies appear.

1908 The Wednesday Psychological Society takes a new name: the Vienna Psychoanalytic Society. On April 26, a congress of Freudian psychology is held in Salzburg, considered the first international congress of psychoanalysis.

1909 Journey to America, at the invitation of Stanley Hall, president of Clark University in Worcester, Massachusetts, together with Jung and Ferenczi.

1910 At the Second Congress of Psychoanalysis (Nuremberg, March 30–31) Jung is elected president of the International Psychoanalytical Association. Bleuler's resignation, which became definitive the following year. Freud publishes *Leonardo da Vinci and a Memory of His Childhood* [*SE*, 11: 59–137]. Meeting with Gustav Mahler.

1911 Founding of the periodical *Imago*, dedicated to nonmedical applications of psychoanalysis. Break with Adler.

1912 Due to internal disagreements, Jones proposes setting up a *committee* of a few trusted analysts, who would deal with the further development of psychoanalysis. It is made up of Jones, Ferenczi, Rank, Sachs, and Abraham. It assumes its proper functions, in practice, after the war.

1912–1913 Freud writes *Totem and Taboo* [*SE*, 13: 1–161]. "Since *The Interpretation of Dreams* I have not worked at anything with such certainty and elation. The reception will be the same."

1913 Final break with Jung.

1914   Faced with war, Freud has an immediate reaction of patriotic enthusiasm, which lasts no more than fifteen days. A few months later he writes to Abraham that helplessness and misery, which do not seem very distant, are the things he has always hated the most. He publishes "On Narcissism: An Introduction" [*SE*, 14: 74–102], which causes notable confusion among his followers due to the modifications in the theory of instincts it presents.

1915   From March to August he writes ten "meta-psychological" essays, seven of which, according to Jones, were subsequently destroyed.

1917   Freud prints the second part of the *Introductory Lectures on Psychoanalysis* [*SE*, 15–16]. During a train journey he writes "A Childhood Recollection from *Dichtung und Wahrheit*" [*SE*, 17: 145–156].

1919   Founding of a private publishing house, the Internationaler Psychoanalytischer Verlag. In October Freud is awarded the title of full professor at the University of Vienna.

1920   Death of Toni von Freund, promoter of the Verlag and, three days later, of Freud's daughter Sophie. Opening of the Berlin Psychoanalytic Polyclinic. He publishes *Beyond the Pleasure Principle* [*SE*, 18: 7–64], begun in 1919.

1921   He publishes *Group Psychology and the Analysis of the Ego* [*SE*, 18: 67–143], conceived simultaneously with *Beyond the Pleasure Principle*. Freud's work and name become more and more well-known. André Gide asks for permission to publish his writings in the *Nouvelle Revue Française*. Visit of André Breton, founder of the surrealist movement.

1922   Berlin Congress, the last congress at which Freud is present.

1923   A cancerous proliferation appears on his palate, and Freud undergoes the first of the thirty-three interventions that will later become necessary. In the same period, the death of Heinerle, the son of Sophie, for whom he had a particular tenderness. He publishes *The Ego and the Id* [*SE*, 19: 3–66].

1924   Rank breaks with Freud.

1925   Death of Karl Abraham.

1926   First meeting with Albert Einstein. Publishes *Inhibitions, Symptoms and Anxiety* [*SE*, 20: 77–174].

1927   Disagreements with Ferenczi. He publishes *The Future of an Illusion* [*SE*, 21: 3–56].

1929   *Civilization and Its Discontents* [*SE*, 21: 59–145].

1930   On the initiative of the poet Alfons Paquet and the novelist Alfred Döblin, he is awarded the Goethe prize. Death of his mother. "I was not free to die as long as she was alive, and now I can." Beginning of the exodus of analysts to America.

1932 The economic situation of the publishing house becomes difficult, and Freud appeals to the International Psychoanalytical Association to take over responsibility for it in the future. In March he receives the first visit from Thomas Mann. Ferenczi's psychic balance begins significantly to alter, and this leads to a personal estrangement. In response to a letter from Einstein, Freud writes "Why War?" [*SE*, 22: 197–215], published by the League of Nations.

1933 "The Nazis' systematic suppression of the Jews, depriving them of all positions, has as yet scarcely begun. . . . The world is turning into an enormous prison. Germany is the worst cell." In May, his books are burned in Berlin. "What progress we are making. In the Middle Ages they would have burnt me." Ferenczi's psychic condition, connected to a state of pernicious anemia, worsens; he dies in May.

1934 "In view of the recent ordinances one asks oneself again how Jews have become what they are, and why they have drawn on to themselves such undying hatred." He begins to write *Moses and Monotheism* [*SE*, 23: 3–137], on a subject that "persecuted him throughout his life."

1937 The first two parts of *Moses* appear in *Imago*.

1938 After the invasion of Austria by the Nazis, Freud finally agrees to leave. A permit is granted to him through the intervention of American diplomacy and—it seems—of Mussolini. He leaves on June 4 and a few days later, in London, writes to Max Eitingon: "The triumphant feeling of liberation is mingled too strongly with mourning, for one had still very much loved the prison from which one has been released." Salvador Dalí pays a visit. In August his book on Moses is released in Amsterdam.

1939 The cancer Freud fought against for sixteen years now becomes inoperable. "My world is what it was previously: a small island of pain floating on a sea of indifference." He dies shortly after midnight on September 23.

A Conquistador

On June 4, 1938, at eighty-two years of age, Sigmund Freud left Vienna permanently for London. Psychoanalysis had already for some years almost disappeared from

Central Europe; already in May of 1933 Freud's books had been burned, in Berlin, as a supreme example of "Jewish" and "non-German" culture.

Freud had been ill with cancer for fifteen years.

Crossing the Channel, at night, he had a brief dream which he told to one of his sons the morning after. "I dreamt of disembarking at Pevensey." Receiving a puzzled response, he had to explain to his son that the person who had disembarked at Pevensey, in 1066, was William the Conqueror.

The exhausted man, who arriving in London would say of himself "I am an old Jew," thus conserved the impulse of the *Conqueror*, or better, of the *Conquistador* inside himself ("I am by temperament, nothing but a *conquistador*—an adventurer, if you want it translated"), which he had been for a good part of his life.

The Archaeology of the Banal

The *Conquistador* had also manifested itself more fully on other occasions.

In 1909, shortly before disembarking in New York, on the only journey he made to the United States, Freud turned to Jung, saying to him in a somewhat prophetic manner: "They don't realize that we're bringing them the plague." Still earlier, in 1897, in perhaps the most critical moment of his research on neurotics, when his theory of the genesis of hysterical disturbances, which he had believed for years, was demonstrated to be unsustainable, he wrote to his friend Fliess: "It is curious that I feel not in the least disgraced, though the occasion might seem to require it. Certainly I shall not tell it in Gath, or publish it in the streets of Askalon, in the land of the Philistines—but between ourselves, I have the feeling more of triumph than of defeat." Even before this—we know it from the *Interpretation of Dreams*—in his bleak Viennese childhood, he had dreamed of the marshal Masséna's baton, the only Jew, as is said, among Napoleon's generals . . .

At this point, one might ask why we bundle together data scattered across seventy-eighty years of life; and what it means that behind the most well-known image of Freud, as the mild-mannered "interpreter" of neurosis, we see the image of Freud emerge as a general, whom he had dreamt of becoming as a boy.

In a certain sense, the response we can give to this question today, like the question itself, contains an essential aspect of Freud's innovation in the world of culture. Finding the past in the present and vice versa, the aggressive element in passivity and vice versa, collecting together, that is, two antithetical terms of a conflict deep-rooted in humanity—this constitutes perhaps the core of the psychoanalytic method.

Yet this method cannot be understood fully if not through the singularity of the person of Freud. The relationship between the creator and his work is in this case fairly close to the link of carnal filiation, so to speak, which is established between the writer and his book, between the artist and his painting, and not to the indirect connection between the scientist and his discovery. There is something unrepeatable which forever confers onto the Freudian construction a character of cultural *unicum*, and generates the ever-recurring difficulty of "placing" it positively among the other sciences. What Freud has left us cannot be cataloged easily; it does not enter into the habitual schemata, even if it is often referred to these.

Precisely for this reason, it does not even enter into the laws of artistic creation. Freud searched in himself— and we will see soon to what extent this searching is literally unheard-of—but in a direction which is frankly the least "artistic" in the classical sense, and not in the slightest sublimatory. He searched in himself for the traces of the banal, of what is common to everyone; he interrogated himself over his mistakes, his tics, his dreams, we would say almost over the drowsy expressions of the alert mind, the slight surfacing impulses that a centuries-old habit toward our idealization of ourselves and our world has led us to consider dross, the dead residue of our childhood.

He had, that is, absolute faith in what intellectual pride scorned, and still scorns, and not for nothing has he often been accused of having created "psychiatry for little women," when he has not been taken for a kabbalist of dreams.

In this sense, the sole legitimate-enough predecessor that we can find for him is neither a writer nor a scientist, but a man whose books he knew and who returns here and there in his writings. This is Heinrich Schliemann, the ingenuous as much as fortunate discoverer of the city of Troy. Like Freud, Schliemann had faith in his own childhood, in the promise made as a child to his father who read him the *Iliad*: "When I grow up, I will discover this city." Forty years later, trusting absolutely in Homer, that is, in his own childhood, he adventurously discovered the old and loved city among the swamps of the Troad. ("My claims are extremely modest. I do not hope to find masterpieces of the plastic arts. The only goal of my excavations has from the beginning been that of recovering the old city of Troy.") Freud ran the same truly *foolish* risk, in our eyes: at a certain point in his life, from within a cultural formation which was among the most rigid, he began to trust in the prehistoric residues of his childhood, in that condemned part of us that returns in dreams and fantasies.

A Victorian Model

For this reason, too, it is difficult to speak of Freud. Or perhaps it is more correct to say that Freud precisely has taught us to see distinctly the limits and inexhaustibly generic quality of every biographical attempt which aspires to be *knowledge* of the subject. In 1936, "frightened by the threat" of Arnold Zweig "becoming his biographer," Freud wrote him some lines by now very well known: "Anyone turning biographer commits himself to lies, to concealment, to hypocrisy, to flattery, and even to hiding his own lack of understanding, for biographical truth is not to be had, and even if it were it couldn't be used. Truth is unobtainable; humanity does not deserve it." Let us omit for now this last, bitter accent, and also the curious contradiction of the man who wanted, many times, and above all in *Leonardo da Vinci and a Memory of His Childhood*, to penetrate into the personal world of another on the basis of few indications—and who should thus fall under the indictment without appeal reserved for biographers. We ask ourselves instead what "biographical truth" is for and after Freud, as it is difficult, if not impossible, to possess. If we read his analysis of writers and artists, or better yet his clinical cases, the psychological fact (whatever it may be) seems to acquire little by little a consistency and stability similar to that in a case of experimental observation. What can be noted, however, with as much evidence is the patient work of subsequent penetration, layer after layer, with the addition of new information, through which every element discovered, which at the outset has the hardness of metal, is corroded little by little, and allows a new situation to shine through which brings it together with other elements. We realize then, too, that in Freud the truth is the *work* of the truth—as much as his observations on artists or patients were certainly not confirmed, but were developed, brought forward, to a point that Freud had only just, or had not even, foreseen. The "biographical truth" of which he speaks in his response to Zweig is also of this nature. Certainly it is not a crystalized fact, made fetish, whatever its origin may be, but the movement itself of an approach toward a person, in which his contradictory relationships with those things that surround him and have inhabited him are gradually defined. This is also probably one of the few legitimate modes of approaching the founder of psychoanalysis and evaluating his work. In the last decades, besides the fundamental biography by Ernest Jones, we have had isolated contributions and critical studies; but at the same time a vast institutional silence has come into being, destined, it would seem, to reabsorb Freud completely into his work, so as not to be constrained to take interest in personal events and settings which do not coincide with the Olympian image that various psychoanalytic societies have of him. That this caution is accompanied by the danger of a diminished comprehension of his work itself is evident even to those who are not psychoanalysts by profession; it is less evident, perhaps, that the caution is based on the assumption of the "biographical truth" of facts and particulars considered in their own right, isolated, and thus subjected to a dangerous degradation of meaning which we could call positivist.

If now we attempt to *approach* Freud, it seems we have before us a unitary surface which starts to crumble, while new forms emerge, indistinct—an enigmatic face. There is an extrinsic part of his life (not for this any the less *real*), an eminently Victorian aspect of it, so to speak, which confers on him that family resemblance common to many portraits of academics and intellectuals of the nineteenth century. One might almost say that he repeats a life model which was that of his anatomist and physiologist teachers and which will be that of many men of science who come after him, not excluding some of his disciples. Here we are alluding not only to his truly untiring industriousness and the meaning this assumes as an ethical norm in the individual life, but to the style of life, to the (even) fanatical moderation, to the frugal and reserved use of the "goods" of life, which are moreover cautiously evaluated. Freud's motto, as he told those who asked him what he considered important in life, *arbeiten und lieben* (to work and to love), rings out like the epitaph for a well-organized and self-secure bourgeois society, even if it is by now very clear what heterodox, if not in fact sinister, significance must be attributed to the second term in this pairing, following Freud's work itself.

This is his faded aspect—conventional like the gray façade of that house in Vienna, Berggasse 19, where André Breton found him in 1921. Having gone to greet

the spiritual master of the surrealist revolution, Breton
came upon a colorless man, lacking vitality, a tradition-
alist in artistic and literary matters.

Dickens, Childhood

Beyond this life model, itself remade after other models,
it is Freud's childhood which seems to us to have an extraordinarily nineteenth-century appearance.

He is the eldest son (after the departure of his half-
brothers for England) of a half-poor, half-bourgeois
Jewish family, which bets everything on him; as a student, his life is that of a boy who is strenuously preparing himself for a future liberal profession since this
will have to be the repayment for his family's sacrifices.
These are the years spent in a "long and narrow room
separated from the rest of the flat, with a window look-
ing on to the street." "All through the years of his school
and university life," Jones recounts, "the only thing that
changed in it was an increasing number of crowded
bookcases. In his teens he would even eat his evening
meal there so as to lose no time from his studies. He
had an oil lamp to himself, while the other bedrooms
had only candles."

Here there is, in a Dickensian style, the *heroic* core
of a boy who knows that he can only count on culture
to fulfill his feats ahead. Fifty years later, he will pick

up this thread again in a strangely indirect and almost generic memory:

The present time seemed to sink into obscurity and the years between ten and eighteen would rise from the corners of my memory, with all their guesses and illusions, their painful distortions and heartening successes—my first glimpses of an extinct civilization (which in my case was to bring me as much consolation as anything else in the struggles of life), my first contacts with the sciences, among which it seemed open to me to choose to which of them I should dedicate what were no doubt my inestimable services. And I seem to remember that through the whole of this time there ran a premonition of a task ahead, till it found open expression in my school-leaving essay as a wish that I might during the course of my life contribute something to our human knowledge. *Ich bin dann Arzt geworden.*

The conclusion ("Later I became a physician") sounds to our ears curiously flattened, prosaic—like the end of a well-woven tale in which we wonder what the protagonist will ever do now that, after so many hopes and despairs, he has come to rest in a good settled middle-class life, as a married and esteemed doctor.

The Goethean Fragment

Yet already in the choice of the profession of doctor— beyond the predictable family ambitions that were focused on him—there is an unusual note, a more distant and indistinct call. The "happy child of Freiberg," the "favorite son of a young mother" who became the book-loving boy of the Sperl Gymnasium, once said that he felt pushed toward medical studies by the public reading of a fragment, "Nature," inspired if not written directly by Goethe: "Nature! We are surrounded and embraced by her: powerless to separate ourselves from her, and powerless to penetrate beyond her. . . . We live in her midst and know her not. She is incessantly speaking to us, but betrays not her secret. . . . Her crown is love. Through love alone dare we come near her. She separates all existences, and all tend to intermingle. She has isolated all things in order that all may approach one another. She holds a couple of draughts from the cup of love to be fair payment for the pains of a lifetime. . . . She hides under a thousand names and phrases, and yet is always the same."

It is the "noninvestigable, absolute, ironic essence" in whose living divinity we recognize the traces of Goethe's commentary on Spinoza. It is also, *in nuce*, the disquieting mother or sister figure, now angelic, now perverse, now tender, now a destroyer, who wanders through so many of the pages of German romanticism. In the schoolboy still undecided on the choice of science to offer his services to, she was to awaken a distant, fleeting echo, and this was not to be extinguished, since we will see her emerge little by little, with difficulty, in the course of his long years dedicated to scientific and humanistic apprenticeship.

A Materialistic Oath

To put it simply: the discovery of psychoanalysis cannot be understood except through the progressive freeing of a man (and his work) from a world of scientific norms and cultural values that he himself took up in the course of his long education. However, it is necessary to understand the meaning of this liberation precisely. Nothing mythically demiurgic, in the sense of a rigid proposition of goals, along with the conscious rejection of others; the drama unfolds, so to speak, without speaking parts, and the protagonist himself seems to be groping, discovering his own path in the very act wherein he *rediscovers* the buried signs of his previous journey. Not therefore a reflection in one's own interior image, already complete or in preparation; but the surprised questioning that precedes and accompanies the deciphering of an unearthed text.

In this sense, even the scientific route leading from the chaste and fervent lover of an undefined Nature to the highly lucid and mature Freud passes through a kind of gradual wearing through and consumption of each phase of evolution.

His first scholarly communications date back to the university period and deal with problems of comparative anatomy and histology. A fact that is repeatedly noted: after choosing medicine, Freud immediately and for many years distanced himself from clinical research—and from humans. Furthermore, what strikes those who look back at those early exercises today is the effort toward impersonal objectivity, which corresponds quite well to what is usually considered a "scientific style," but which seems to have lost all trace of the emotion in the face of nature once perceived in the Goethean fragment.

One might say that we are confronted with the scholarly accentuation of that antivitalistic attitude, the enemy of Goethean-Schellingian *Naturphilosophie*, which had become the article of faith, moreover an extraordinarily valuable one, of the generation of physiologists which the young Freud approached.

This is the famous materialistic "oath" of the Helmholtz school, as Jones summarizes it: "Organisms differ from dead material entities in action—machines—in possessing the faculty of assimilation, but they are all phenomena of the physical world; systems of atoms, moved by forces, according to the principle of the conservation of energy discovered by Robert Mayer in 1842, neglected for twenty years and then popularized by Helmholtz. . . . The real causes are symbolized in science by the word 'force.' . . . Progress in knowledge reduces them to two—attraction and repulsion. All this applies as well to the organism man."

There has long been an insistence on this materialistic, mechanistic sheath worn by Freud at the time of his scientific apprenticeship and jealously safeguarded by him, until his last days, against any spiritualist "temptation."

However, we would run the risk of being totally tendentious in pointing Freud solely in this direction, as did the first critiques of phenomenological origin. The image of a profound maternal nature, living and intimate to man, into which his vocation for science is translated as its origin, as we have seen, always coexists with his subsequent intellectual setting; concealed, repressed, submissive, it will prove invincible. In this sense, one could speak of a specific Freudian *chiaroscuro* which cannot be eliminated from his work, from which increasingly intimate and distant figures emerge little by little.

The student tasked with examining the testicles of eels, or the spinal cord of *Ammocoetes petromyzon*, the young neurologist who is tireless in his observations under the microscope, embodies a "labor of the intellect" that kills and dissects living nature. But the echo this labor finds in the young anatomist is already significant. "I am preparing myself for my real profession," he writes to a friend, W. Knöpfmacher, "'flaying of animals or torturing of human beings,' and I find myself more and more in favor of the former." In the form of a paradoxical joke, what emerges here is not only the repugnance toward the body which is so frequent among medical students and which must be exorcised with macabre mockery, the anatomy room joke. Science is also experienced as torture, as a rupture of the body—with an overturning of positions, an insistence on the penetrating aspect, the aspect of the (quite forced) abstract cruelty of the cognitive act, which reveals a subsequent crisis. The little concern that Freud showed, in 1882, at having to give up a career as a researcher in the physiology institute headed by E. Brücke, apparently caused by economic difficulties, cannot be explained otherwise. This renunciation comes at the same moment as his decision to finally accept the profession of doctor, a figure who *treats* his patients.

How the Spirit Will Heal Itself

At this point, Freud's story seems to be entirely resolved in a series of classic chapters, linked together by a purely intellectual thread, on which the protagonist himself has constantly insisted in his sober autobiographies. In 1885, attracted by the international fame of Charcot's neurological school, he goes to Paris on a scholarship and attends the Salpêtrière, where the French master has carried out a prodigious reevaluation of hysteria, which until then had been considered by doctors and the family members of hysterics as little more, or not much less, than a conscious mystification of the subject. In the hospital where Pinel had unchained the insane, "Charcot, in a small way, renewed the act of liberation remembered by the painting . . . hanging on the wall," establishing the reality of hysterical phenomena, their presence in the male sex too, and producing paralysis and contractures through hypnotic suggestion similar to those of the disease. *Hysterical disorders are essentially caused by psychic mechanisms.*

Back in Vienna, Freud is forced to use the only two tools within the therapeutic arsenal of the time— electrotherapy and hypnosis—to treat the neurotics who make up the vast majority of his meager clientele. He quickly realizes that electrotherapy functions only by the effect of suggestion; hypnosis has at least the advantage of apparently freeing the doctor "from the feeling of his impotence" and flattering him with "the reputation of obtaining miraculous cures." In order to perfect his hypnotic technique, to whose shortcomings he attributes his own setbacks, he goes to Nancy in 1889, where Liébault and Bernheim use hypnosis for therapeutic purposes on a large scale. He is particularly struck by the experiments with *posthypnotic suggestion*: a subject has been given a particular task during hypnosis, with the suggestion to forget the order given. Once awake, he performs it as a spontaneous act, without remembering its origin. However, if you insist that he remember the order he was given, he often succeeds: it is thus demonstrated that *the motives behind our acts are not always known to us, although it is possible to make these conscious with particular effort.*

Hypnosis, however, does not satisfy Freud, since it gives results that are sometimes flashy but transitory and that in any case affect only the symptom, the most superficial manifestation, but not the morbid "mechanism." He therefore decides to repeat the very unique therapeutic attempt of which his friend Dr. Joseph Breuer had informed him in 1883, even before his stay in Paris. This concerned a girl, Anna O., whom Breuer had treated for a few years due to a complex hysterical case history. By chance, Breuer realized that by letting the girl freely express the fantasies that went through her mind, her state improved significantly. He had therefore decided to subject the girl to hypnotic sessions, during which he invited her to freely communicate whatever was oppressing her at that moment. In this way, a very clear connection was established between each apparently incomprehensible symptom and a vivid impression aroused by a past event, which in her waking state she did not remember. The event of *reliving* this impression during hypnosis, through the reemergence of the forgotten incident, was enough to make the symptom itself disappear: hence the name of *cathartic* method was given to the curious therapeutic procedure employed by Breuer, or *talking cure*, or the "chimney sweeping" method, a name given by the patient. Freud therefore begins to use hypnosis only as a means to resurrect these impressions, of which the waking patient is unaware, which seem to be at the origin of her symptoms. After having collected numerous personal observations, he convinces the reluctant Breuer to publish with him, in 1893, a preliminary communication entitled "On the Psychical Mechanism of Hysterical Phenomena: Preliminary Communication" and two years later, in 1895, the *Studies on Hysteria*, to which the birth of psychoanalysis is officially traced.

In the meantime, however, he has already gone much further than Breuer. The state of hypnosis, on which the cathartic reevocation seems to be based, is not obtained in many patients, or is obtained to an insufficient extent; moreover, it is accompanied by a very intense personal relation to the doctor, which cannot be controlled. He therefore decides to give it up and limit himself to a technique of *concentration*: the patient, lying on a couch with her eyes closed, is invited to communicate what she remembers about the symptom she wants to eliminate; if nothing comes to the surface, the doctor places a hand on her forehead, suggesting that now an idea will surely come to her mind—precisely the one she searches for. In this way, Freud draws upon Bernheim's experiments mentioned previously: *the patient knows—without knowing that she knows—the origin of her illness; it is a question of bringing it back to consciousness, of forcing it to reveal itself.* However, this forcing will be obtained, paradoxically, by gradually renouncing, after hypnosis, any form of solicitation, suggestion, or concentration. "Instead of urging the patient to say something upon some particular subject, I now asked him to abandon himself to a process of free association—that is, to say whatever came into his head, while ceasing to give any conscious direction to his thoughts. It was essential, however, that he should bind himself to report literally everything that occurred to his self-perception and not to give way to critical objections which sought to put certain associations on one side on the ground that they were not sufficiently important or that they were irrelevant or that they were altogether meaningless."

This is Freud's "soaring at his highest," which made Breuer say he "gaze[d] after him as a hen at a hawk." Neurosis, from now on, will speak in the first person, and to understand it, the doctor will simply have to try to *grasp every word, since every word is significant.*

It is not of interest here to look for the innumerable historical and cultural roots of this fundamental innovation, as they have already been identified several times. Each of these roots must pass through a center: the person of Freud himself, as through the slow change developing in him during these years; so much so that it is not possible to give a precise date for his "technical innovation"—the method of "free association." At first glance, and superficially, the method is the triumph of the mechanistic determinism that constituted the oath of the Helmholtz school: everything is rigidly produced by well-determined causes. Yet, more deeply, if we retrace the slow path that goes from hypnotic submission to waking suggestion to active concentration, we see the *object* of treatment emerge: *neurosis*, as part of a naturalistic catalog, becomes a human *subject*, which contains its own meaning within itself. At the same time, Freud renounces any instrument of direct intervention that might seem the agent of resolution. He almost becomes passive and distant, a patient listener to a nature "incessantly speaking to us," as the Goethean fragment of his adolescence has it.

Resistance, Unconscious, Sex

This is a nature that at one and the same time—and it must be said forcefully against any ecstatic vision— "betrays not her secret" to us, except through hard toil, continuous *work*. Faced with a void that only the analyst's gaze traverses, the subject immediately breaks the accepted rule of saying everything: in infinite ways he shuns, objects, is silent, or speaks so as not to speak— he *resists*, he refuses to give voice to painful or shameful areas of his life. There is therefore someone or something who, contradictorily, *defends himself* against the coming to light of a rejected part, which he keeps hidden from clear consciousness, a "defensive mechanism" that is manifested through this resistance. Hence Freud's conclusion: this presently opposed "force," acting as resistance to the flow of associations and ultimately to transforming the morbid state, must be the same force that generated this state.

At the origin of the neurosis there is therefore a struggle, a conflict between opposing elements; the losing side has been removed from consciousness but continually presses to return to it. Whenever there is a rupture in the balance, the repressed element returns; however, given that the barrier opposing it does not yield completely, it is expressed through compromise formations—the symptoms—which precariously satisfy the two warring parties.

Here we stand before the key nexus of Freudian insight, on which the whole immense construction will later rest. It is essential to note how it comes to light, with all of its implications, and finds the foundation of its scientific truth—that is, first of all, the possibility of repetition and control—in the experimental situation devised by Freud for the treatment of neurotics.

Thus, the *unconscious*. It can no longer be defined as a mystical place or receptacle of a deep will or wisdom, the night of the universal soul—as in the thinkers whom Freud has often been put alongside: Schopenhauer, Carus, von Hartmann. Instead it is essentially constituted in relation to a *refusal*, as what the subject denies to his own life and consciousness and which, in being denied, continues to exist and reaffirm itself. As what, finally, can be revealed only through patient work that overcomes the originary refusal. What is rejected, removed from consciousness, is an experimental finding, so to speak, linked to the history of the individual patient (and, as such, to the history of all others). However, it is true that sociohistorical variability is at the same time slow-moving and relatively constant. For this reason, we can still find the same "amazement" within ourselves with which Freud looked upon the mutilated, trampled being, emerging slowly, from beyond the barrier of consciousness, which we are forced to call a *body*, with its needs, desires, and ramified fantasies. To this tangle of relations, which would prove to be extraordinarily complicated, he gave the name *sexuality*, thus unleashing a historical scandal that would prove as vast and necessary in the immediate term as, in the long run, it would be a source of ambiguity and limitation. In fact, Freud is not a sexologist à la Havelock Ellis or Krafft-Ebing, who were his esteemed contemporaries, or à la Kinsey, to give an example closer to our time. Sexual desire, strictly speaking, which his research collides with and which he is forced to name, is the point of final convergence of a series of disaggregated elements, which come almost gushing forth from the human organism in its phase of development, expressing its tendency to pleasure. In this sense, it is fair to say that Freud "desecrated" childhood innocence, following the incredibly weak accusation of contemporary hypocrisy; but he did so only to restore to adult sexuality, either normal or deviant, a sense of totally expressing the individual life, in which the hindrances and hidden violence suffered since childhood are clearly reflected.

Reaching this point was not easy—and not because of the violent and superficial ostracism to which Freud fell victim. It was the notion of sexuality itself that had to be overthrown.

The cathartic method, as we have seen, seemed to presuppose the discovery of a specific *traumatic event*, an episode unbearable for the patient's waking personality and therefore removed from consciousness, repressed. The need for an episode of this kind—in which the positivistic fetish of the *data* is condensed, deriving from Charcot's teaching on so-called traumatic hysteria—remains in Freud even by the time he has fully developed the method of free association. Since the neurotic's principal defenses concern the sexual sphere itself, it will be necessary to try to reach the *sexual trauma* seemingly at the origin of his disturbances; the nature of this episode, together with the subject's way of reacting, probably determine the type of neurosis developed. This is the thesis of the sexual seduction of a child by an adult (most usually a person within his family), which Freud erroneously generalizes based on observations of some patients, giving support to this thesis between 1893 and 1897. Sexuality is still the dirty laundry of adults, and Freud blushes "about as much as patients in general" when forced to confront certain topics.

Self-Analysis

The decisive turning point comes when this neurologist, aged almost forty, prematurely graying, a father of six, begins to explore himself with the aid of his new method. Formally, it seems to be facing that movement, classic within the history of culture, whereby a lost truth searches for itself and finds itself *within* man. However, a fundamental difference immediately strikes us. Freud's research is from the start anti-aristocratic, devoid of any privilege or superiority based on pride. He tries to turn himself into a simple listener to himself, letting the trampled-upon, rejected part reappear, as in his neurotic patients. "All of what I experienced with my patients, as a third person I find again here—days when I drag myself about dejected because I have understood nothing of the dream, of the fantasy, of the mood of the day; and then again days when a flash of lightning illuminates the interrelations and lets me understand the past as a preparation for the present." At another point: "Many a sad secret of life is here followed back to its first roots; many a pride and privilege are made aware of their humble origins." Literally, Freud becomes his own *patient*, with a lucidity that will later appear even inhuman, and not unreasonably ("The chief patient I am preoccupied with is myself").

In this way, a continuous exchange is established between what he learns from his patients and what he draws from himself. If he once wrote, "I always find it uncanny when I can't understand someone in terms of myself," now he can complete the thought: "I can only analyze myself with objectively acquired knowledge (as if I were a stranger)."

Since neurotics often encounter themselves, in the course of analysis, in some of their dreams, and these dreams reveal themselves to be directly related to their problems—that is, implying a meaning of *desire*, albeit distorted and masked—Freud takes note of his dreams and tries to understand, through his method, the rules of interpretation.

It is a moment of unspeakable "intellectual beauty"— for the first time, reason explores what apparently has always opposed it as anti-reason: the chaotic world of the night which, populated by "angels and spiritual servants," according to Paracelsus, has always been felt, in the words of Novalis, as our most secret "homeland."

In fact, the angels—and monsters—that populate this night little by little reveal themselves to be familiar. Vague reproaches emerge, someone or something accuses Freud of not curing his patients, of not taking an interest in his colleagues and his family, while he defends himself, inventing justifications. Paradoxically, the strongest desire that he finds within himself, under the closed-over husk of dreams, is that of ridding himself of a still indistinct guilt. The interpretation, however, is *surrounded by enormous and obstinate sphinxes* and seems to want to lead to the paralysis of every other capacity. It is the death of his father, Jacob, in October 1896, which transforms this intellectual adventure into something that will more deeply involve Freud. At first, the death does not seem to affect Freud very significantly; his father is an eighty-one-year-old who has been ill for some time; in his letters, Freud enumerates with scientific precision and apparent indifference the causes that led him to his end. But almost immediately the picture changes. "By one of those dark pathways behind the official consciousness the old man's death has affected me deeply. . . . By the time he died, his life had long been over, but in my inner self the whole past has been reawakened by this event." The night after his father's funeral, Freud has a brief dream, which condenses into a vision of a bizarre sign: *You are requested to close the eyes.* Closing the eyes of his dead father is a filial duty Freud fulfilled—but he arrived late to the funeral, and his family was displeased with him because he wanted everything to happen in a merely "simple and silent" way. The dream is therefore also an invitation to indulgence: close your eyes on *my* guilt. The latter is therefore outlined as a *guilt toward the father*—of whom the colleagues, friends, and family members introduced in previous dreams are only more or less distant copies, figures of substitution. At the same time, a position of resentment, of hidden hostility, seems to emerge among the meshes of thoughts knotted around the tragic double sense of the dream, which has managed to express itself in his

inattentions so acutely felt by family members (he arrived late to the funeral, he did everything so austerely).

In the following months—in a period of strenuous
work, fertile with new observations and hypotheses—
Freud continues this discourse with the dead through
the screen of dreams, in which he is both accused and
accuser. A situation of affective conflict worsens: a con-
suming tenderness and nostalgia, which surprises the
dreamer himself, is inevitably accompanied, as if by a
necessary counterstep, by increasingly violent and explicit accusations. In a dream, he comes to accuse old Jacob of what for Freud was always on the surface a motive
for his open pride: being a *Jew*, having begotten a *Jew*,
for which reason Freud will forever be denied becoming a university professor in the anti-Semitic milieu of
Vienna. Further still: the theory of the child's sexual seduction by an adult, which in the surrounding years, as
we have seen, has been at the center of his interpretation
of the neuroses, touches for a moment the venerable
figure of Jacob.

In April 1897, a hysteric woman tells him at length
what her father, a man "otherwise noble and respect-
able," did to her as a child. Freud comments laconically:
Quod erat demonstrandum. In May, he has a dream in
which *his own* erotic desire for his daughter Mathilde
seems to appear: here, therefore, is the supreme confirmation of his theory, which indicates that the father
is responsible for the neurosis of the child. I, Sigmund,

am guilty toward my daughter, as you, Jacob, are guilty toward me. And so we come to the summer of 1897, in which Freud finds himself disoriented before this dead man and before himself, unable to find the interpretive key to their relationship. He undergoes "some kind of neurotic experience, curious states incomprehensible to Cs. [consciousness], twilight thoughts, veiled doubts, with barely a ray of light here or there." "I have never before even imagined anything like this period of intellectual paralysis. Every line is torture." The situation seems stuck in the gestures of a child who accuses his father of having corrupted him. The solution will come after months and months of agonizing hesitation, and will repeat the most characteristic movement of Freud's genius once again. The increasingly bitter accusations against the father actually cover over—though *less and less*—the emergence of images and dreams, now indistinct, now tumultuous, in which an extraordinary *fantastical* world is reflected, of Freud as a child and his contradictory desire toward his parents. As before, with the tremor of the witness, he listened to the accusations defaming his father, now he knows how to listen to the buried, disturbing story of himself as a child. Not the father's desire, but the child as *a being of desire*, is at the origin of the neurosis. It is not a story of adult seduction, but the groping attempts to move toward the adult; that confused magma of love-hate for the father and the mother which finds in the myth of Oedipus Rex—killer of his father and husband of his mother—its first, illuminating definition. "Everyone in the audience was once a budding Oedipus in fantasy and each recoils in horror from the dream fulfilment here transplanted into reality."

Oedipus and His Father

As if in the shards of a broken mirror, the real face of little Sigi and his parents recomposes itself in this way through dreams and memories. That extraordinary chastity or sexual frigidity which, when he becomes an adult, will amaze his friends and enemies breaks down precisely at its origin and lets us glimpse the voracious childhood curiosities on which it is built—and, moreover, those that he finds in his patients. In the obscurity of his early childhood, the nudity of his mother appears for a moment, Amalia who is just over twenty years old, wife of a man twice her age. This latter man changes his face: he is no longer the little "luckless" Galician merchant, always on the verge of bankruptcy, as full of jokes as he is unable to provide stably for the needs of his family, the man who in Sigmund's adolescence will bitterly recall the image of the Dickensian Mr. Micawber, that "talker" who was always "transported with grief and mortification" before his creditors, and who, however, "within half an hour afterward . . . would polish up his shoes with extraordinary pains, and go out, humming a tune with a greater air of gentility than ever." And he is not even just the man—so similar to Garibaldi!—who tells his ten-year-old son how once, in Freiberg, a Christian slapped him, ordering him to get off the sidewalk and throwing his cap into the mud. "And what did you do?"—"I went to the roadway and picked up my cap." (Sigmund promises himself that he will *never* pick up *his* cap.) Further back still, in the close-knit circle of the family world, the figure of his father becomes curiously contradictory. On the one hand, he commands, guides: he is therefore the usurper of Oedipus. Yet in another respect, he seems distant, absent; a patriarchal figure and at the same time purely decorative. Appearing in Freud's memory more vividly and strongly is the figure of Emanuel, the son of Jacob's first marriage, who is about the same age as Amalia, Sigmund's mother, and Emanuel's son, John—younger than Sigmund—whose uncle he also is. Oedipus therefore does not very well know who his father is, who the usurper is: paradoxically, Freud realizes the myth more deeply than any other man: even before killing his father, he *goes in search of* him.

It is necessary to say that even before reaching this conclusion, Freud fell silent, thus making any reconstruction hypothetical. There seems no doubt, however, that here lies one of the secret points of awareness that allowed him at last to resolve, beyond the relationship with his father, and simultaneous to this, the extraordinarily intense bond periodically established with a figure who is at once a friend, an inspiration, a rescuer.

Firstly, with Joseph Breuer, the discoverer of the cathartic method; but above all, with Wilhelm Fliess, a Berlin doctor who in the crucial period of self-analysis plays an essential part, first as a witness and later as a party to the dispute. In a letter of July 1897, Freud writes to him: "I still do not know what has been happening in me. Something from the deepest depths of my own neurosis set itself against any advance in the understanding of the neuroses, and you have somehow been involved in it." He will go far beyond this *I still do not know*; he once again will discover in himself what is obscurely revealed in the treatment of patients too. It is not the meticulous research of and dating of one's past that in itself provides the interpretive key and allows one to overcome its dead remnants, which have survived in the present. It is instead the dialogue arising between the patient and the doctor, their working together, almost blindly, that is at first indistinct, then gradually clearer, becoming more intimate, in which all of the voices of the past converge and are recognized. I believe that I must search for my own private archaeological museum underground—and little by little I see that it opens up to the full light of my own present and the present of my witness.

Moses Is an Egyptian

Freud can now say of himself, like Montaigne in his *Essais*, what few men can fully say: that he has no more made his book than his book has made him. *The Interpretation of Dreams*, which comes out at the end of 1899, is the fundamental text of the new psychological science and, dare we say, of the new *reason*; at the same time, without contradiction, it is born as "a portion of my own self-analysis, my reaction to my father's death—that is to say, to the most important event, the most poignant loss, of a man's life." Like *The Psychopathology of Everyday Life*, which is slightly later, it is truly a book "consubstantial with its author," unrepeatable; if the development of psychoanalysis—as a constituted science and movement within culture—is still all to follow, it is, however, certain that Freud will never again have, as he writes in the third chapter of *The Interpretation of Dreams*, the liberating consciousness of "passing through a narrow defile" to "emerge upon a piece of high ground, where the path divides" and to be "in the full daylight of a sudden discovery." A kind of prolonged childhood, a delay in facing oneself, has ended. But the accounts are *never* closed; in this respect, even the analysis that Freud conducts on himself is truly *unendlich*, interminable. It is true that from now on we will no longer find, or find only infrequently, its direct expression in his writings; we will have to read it in them and through them, as if, paradoxically, the truth has again veiled itself, has once again taken on modes of allusion and concealment. Only his delays and hesitations will show us its scattered traces. Thus, in the alternations of enthusiasm and distrust that accompany the drafting of *Totem and Taboo* (from 1913), we find the echo, if not the repetition, of the difficulties encountered during the work of the years 1896–1897; and the same is true of the obsessive proof he required for the hypotheses he set out in the essay "The Moses of Michelangelo" (from 1914), and finally of the repentances, the justifications, the recommencements which succeed one another all throughout *Moses and Monotheism*, published in 1938 in Amsterdam, a few months before his death.

Decades later, it is not difficult for us to grasp the personal roots of this never-resolved inhibition. In *Totem and Taboo*, the distressing revelation of the tragedy of Oedipus, which Freud experienced in the first person, is simply displaced to the origins of man, becoming the originary drama of the killing of the father of the primal horde, whom each of the killers then makes a beloved and feared model: "After they had got rid of him, had satisfied their hatred and had put into effect their wish to identify themselves with him, the affection which had all this time been pushed under was bound to make itself felt. It did so in the form of remorse." In the meticulous essay dedicated to the *Moses* by Michelangelo, the insistence on the interpretation of the statue's stance and the characteristic uncertainty about its possible meaning betray a perennial difficulty in entering fully into the role of a father, after having been a

child in conflict with his own father for so long. His last
book, that "far from despicable farewell" given by the
"old Jew" to his contemporaries at the moment when
the great massacre began, clarifies conflicts of ambivalence about *being Jewish* that existed in Jacob's son right
from the initial hypothesis—"to take from a people the
man it celebrates as the greatest of its sons," making
Moses an Egyptian. It is almost trivial to say that while
the preparation for the extermination of his people was
under way, Freud helplessly dreamed of putting himself at their head like the ancient leader and of bringing
them to the "good and spacious land" (Exodus 3:8).[84] In
this, he is a fellow and comrade to the young Jews who
a few years later, in Warsaw and Treblinka, would die
fighting, refusing the age-old resignation of their fa-
thers. His identification with Moses also arises from a
refusal—to pick up the cap that a Christian ripped from
his father's head many years before—exactly as Moses'
vocation arises from a rebellion against age-old servi-
tude ("When Moses had grown up, he went out to his
kinsfolk and witnessed their labors. *He saw an Egyptian
beating a Hebrew, one of his kinsmen . . . he struck down
that Egyptian and hid him in the sand*." [Exodus 2:12]). But
this refusal of the position of the father—in order to be
able to save him—seems somehow to imply a passage
to the position of the persecutor, a *becoming-Egyptian*,
which Freud has the extreme honesty to confess, albeit

through the meshes of the hesitant historico-religious discourse he unfolds.

Myth and Civilization

We must therefore ask ourselves what drives Freud, in the last decades, to this mythical-symbolic transcription of himself and his knowledge. He seems to be forced to resort more and more often to evocation, to an *image* that suggests something indirectly. In his way of proceeding, we perceive some awkwardness, uncertainty—and at the same time a hint toward a truth that surpasses Freud the person, even though it involves him.

It is his relationship with the sphere of culture that becomes increasingly complicated. In his everyday work, he continues to produce culture, precisely through those things that traditional culture considers *déchets*, litter left wasting away in illness—or in the irrational. At the same time, and inversely, his continuous reference to the opacity of childhood, to that destiny of hesitation and bewilderment that weighs on the individual man, introduces in culture a moment of criticism, of the suspicion of origin, so to speak, from which he will no longer be able to free himself. From here is born also that infamous movement of the "reduction" of the sublime to the commonplace, and of illusion to its root of impotence, which in its immediate crudeness still maintains the meaning of a preliminary ironic reserve in the face of any abstract value. Freud was perfectly aware of this continually desublimatory and depreciative sense implied in his work. In a 1936 reply to Ludwig Binswanger, who had sent him a copy of one of his speeches given at the Akademischer Verein für Medizinische Psychologie, we find written: "On reading it I enjoy your beautiful diction, your erudition, the scope of your horizon, your tact when contradicting me. You know one can tolerate endless amounts of praise. Naturally I still don't believe you. I have always dwelt only in the ground floor and basement of the building. You assert that, when one changes one's viewpoint, one can also see upper stories in which such distinguished guests as religion, art, etc., reside. You are not the only one in that; most cultivated types of *homo natura* think the same. In that you are the conservative, I am the revolutionary." Here, in fact, irony is essential, the detachment of the viewer from *below*, from the foundations of the building. Here, probably, is also one of the moments of profound affinity with the critique of bourgeois consciousness developed by Marx fifty years earlier, based on the unveiling of another *repression*, the socioeconomic unconscious.

However, at the moment Freud poses to himself the need to return what he has found in himself and his patients to a general context—and this happens, basically, according to a canon of absolute values still at play within him—there arise vacillations and characteristic difficulties. How do we pass from the individual (this one and no other) to the generality of individuals? How do the things uncovered in this individual originate? Freud's first answer—the most "scientific," and the one that a superficial reader constantly finds—is based on an analogy in the first case, and on a (hereditary) transmission in the second. Men *are* the man, the group is the individual, without any sense of delay or mediations that are not directly related to the *single* individual. What is found in the son was in the father and the father's father, through the transfer of traces that are quite inevitably linked to "traumatic" events. It is not relevant here to look at the innumerable objections that this way of proceeding has brought up in sociologists, ethnologists, philosophers. On the other hand, it is interesting to note that it lags somewhat behind the conception of neurosis that Freud elaborates simultaneously. Early humanity experienced *events* which, forgotten, resurface after centuries or millennia of latency: the model he proposes for the history of man therefore seems to involve the notion of childhood trauma which he eliminated from his theory of individual neurosis after the turning point of 1897. With this, the enormous burden of coercions and prohibitions, of habits sedimented in the bedrock of institutions, which humanity carries with it could not find any relief—because of its radical heterogeneity—by learning the "difficulties of life," a process that each individual personally undertakes.

The conceptual tools he uses therefore risk turning out to be partial and misleading in the later development of his research. Although there is no shortage of fruitful sociological successes (for example, *Group Psychology and the Analysis of the Ego*, 1921), the psychoanalysis of civilization—his late task, in which his "original philosophical ambition" seems finally satisfied—might appear simply as an obsessive investigation concerning a prehistoric *fact*, which allows for the eternal return of history as a repressed element.

It will only be the ambiguity of *myth* that will allow him to express, before science and not against it, the new meanings that emerge from his work and for which he is unable to give a precise definition. First of all is the tendency toward destruction, toward the "return to the inorganic," which he sees rising like a deadly cloud in the very heart of civilization, in the period of total wars. The revelation of this tendency—which seems to mark the definitive defeat of that loving nature present in the distant Goethean image—takes place, in *Beyond the Pleasure Principle* (1920), through the discovery of the myth of Eros and Thanatos locked in a continuous and uncertain struggle.

A very tenuous and fragile indication, disarmed; as though, among so many cuirasses and iron breastplates, he gave us a simple thread to follow; but a thread, as Plato recalls, which is as ductile as iron is rigid, because it is a *golden thread*.

Bibliography

Works by Sigmund Freud

These are collected chronologically in the *Gesammelte Werke*, 17 vols. (London: Imago Publishing, 1940–1952) [vol. 18 was published later: Frankfurt am Main: Fischer, 1968]. However, the only critical edition available so far is that in English edited by James Strachey: *The Standard Edition of the Complete Psychological Works of Sigmund Freud*, 24 vols. (London: Hogarth Press, 1953–1974).

Numerous individual works have been published in Italian, especially after World War II, in translations of varying quality. For a preliminary study, we recommend: *La mia vita e psicoanalisi* [My life and psychoanalysis] (Milan: Mursia, 1963); *Psicoanalisi: esposizioni divulgative* [Psychoanalysis: a didactic exposition] (Turin: Boringhieri, 1963); *Introduzione allo studio della psicoanalisi* [Introduction to the study of psychoanalysis] (Rome: Astrolabio, 1948); the *Freud* anthology (Turin: Boringhieri, 1959); *Casi clinici* [Clinical cases] (Turin: Einaudi, 1952); *Inibizione, sintomo e angoscia* [Inhibitions, symptoms, and anxiety] (Turin: Einaudi, 1954). The publisher Boringhieri is currently publishing the complete works; *Lettere 1873–1939* [*Letters of Sigmund Freud: 1873–1939*] (1960) and *Le origini della psicoanalisi. Lettere a Wilhelm Fliess* [*The Origins of Psychoanalysis: Letters to Wilhelm Fliess: 1887–1902*] (1961) have so far been published.

Works on Freud

I have limited myself to Italian works, or those translated into Italian, in which the reader can find further bibliographical references.

The classic exposition of psychoanalysis for Italy is the *Trattato di psicoanalisi* [Treatise on psychoanalysis] by Cesare Luigi Musatti (Turin: Einaudi, 1953); on Freud's life, Ernest Jones, *Vita e opera di Freud* [*The Life and Work of Sigmund Freud*], 3 vols. (Milan: Il Saggiatore, 1962) (from this work I freely drew quotations and references). For the sociological aspects of Freud, *Lezioni di sociologia* [*Aspects of Sociology*], edited by Max Horkheimer and Theodor W. Adorno (Turin: Einaudi, 1966); for the "critique of civilization," *Eros e civiltà* [*Eros and Civilization*], by Herbert Marcuse (Turin: Einaudi, 1964).

Psychoanalysis

1

Having now arrived at the last decades of the twentieth century, it is uncontroversial to recognize, in a rapid profile of psychoanalysis, that this discipline, directly or through techniques derived from it, has reached an almost planetary spread. *Almost*, because there is a notable exception, the world of socialist republics, in which a substantial closure prevails, albeit with notable internal differences: explicit refusal in the USSR, with the alliance between Stalinist Marxism and the Pavlovian tradition; a more nuanced situation in the countries of Eastern Europe, where more recently a somewhat intense revival of interest has become clear.

This diffusion, while certainly enormous, has, however, taken three-quarters of a century to reach its current level. Let us go over its major events. Up until the First World War, psychoanalysis presents itself as an important innovation or oddity ostracized by academic authorities, which has its essential basis in a group of German-speaking Jewish doctors and intellectuals, with significant extensions to some non-Jewish Germanophone centers and to isolated personalities in other countries, in Europe and America. After the First World War, while the ostracism by academia more or less persists, psychoanalysis exits the specialist ambit and consolidates its particular institutions, national and international. With the advent of Nazism, it is expelled from its original centers and finds refuge in the Anglo-Saxon world, where it spreads widely into all cultural spheres. After the Second World War, psychoanalysis, returning to Europe, pervades Western culture and its academic, psychiatric, and psychological institutions to an ever greater degree.

This type of diffusion—wide, but with notable and durable exclusions; slow, but insistent and continuous—allows us perhaps an initial clarification. It is a type of diffusion that recalls the expansion of an ideological movement, or equally of a religion in the traditional sense. It is not the diffusion—possibly delayed, but then rapid and universal—of a strictly scientific discovery. Therefore, in this respect, psychoanalysis is closer to the traditional humanistic disciplines than to, say, molecular biology. The type of science that it claims to constitute thus appears, even from the historical and sociological point of view, different from the natural or biological sciences.

2

Certainly, the theoretical horizon Freud moved within, especially at the outset of his work, was precisely that of the established sciences of his time, through the encounter with the physicalist physiology of von Helmholtz and Brücke, who, in Freud's words, "carried more weight with me than anyone else in my whole life." Yet the working method and the methodology of research which he established rapidly brought him beyond this horizon. Let us turn to certain keystones. Calling on a stranger to express "what occurs in his mind," his own *Einfälle*, Freud demonstrated that he could put entirely between parentheses his neurological-psychiatric understanding of this stranger, whoever it be (and among the first it was Freud *himself*), confident that the truth would be revealed starting from the words of the other. This unprecedented solicitation to expression led to the emergence of a world that, beyond its apparent chaos and the singularity of the individuals in which it emerged, delineated thrusts and tensions discernible in others too. That is, Freud delineated the territory he named the *unconscious*, and its exploration allowed one to know how profound and complex and active, even at a later stage of life, was the continent of *childhood*, which is present in each person. While this exploration, though certainly difficult, could appear at the outset to leave undisturbed the position and the identity of the explorer, it was revealed soon afterward to involve him directly, in the first person. Thus, the concept was born of *transference* (on the part of the person in analysis) and later of *countertransference* (on the part of the analyst): a pair of concepts that is found at the center of psychoanalytic work and discourse.

3

The full promotion of the *Einfälle*, that is to say, the "method of free association"; the revelation through these of the unconscious and the childlike; the elaboration of the analyst-analysand relation as one which overcomes decisively the classic relation of observer-observed: these are some of the fundamental elements of a very distinct experience, in which concordances, replications, and returns emerge and are developed between the often forgotten and distorted past and the present. This is what could be called the solid or weighty nucleus of psychoanalysis, what allowed the Freudian experience to be repeated, confirmed, and contradicted within a specific analytic apparatus or setting that, even in its successive intervening variations, manifests the constancy and uniformity of a specific scientific *laboratory*. It is within this laboratory that the most significant advances of psychoanalysis have taken place—since it is necessary to contest a common notion that is rather widespread, according to which psychoanalysis begins and ends with Freud. It remains true that, insofar as it is the locus of the emergence and enunciation of the unconscious and the childlike, psychoanalysis is found to uncover recurring or typical elements: hence the impression of boredom associated with these in psychoanalytic case studies. Yet it is also true that this territory, after Freud, has known other descriptions, connected on the one hand to the extension of analysis to situations precluded in Freud's time (above all, to children, psychotics, and so-called boundary cases) and on the other hand to a deeper attention turned toward the position of the analyst with respect to the person in analysis and to himself. From this work, in the concrete functioning of the situation between two people, have been derived original conceptualizations which later have entered, in different measures, into the cultured lexicon in general, and which draw legitimacy from their having been born in and inserted into the psychoanalytic laboratory. To take one single example: the process of *identification* with the other in Freud already has a tone and a resonance different from those that it can take in psychiatry and psychology. *Projective* identification, described later by Melanie Klein, came from the expansion of specifically psychoanalytic experience and is intimately linked to it.

4

There is thus a psychoanalytic specificity closely linked to the inauguration of a determinate "experimental" frame. On this there is little disagreement. But disagreement arises as soon as we pass from the plane of repeatable, individual-typical experience to an attempt at general comprehension or explanation of experience itself, of its presuppositions and implications—when, that is, we pose the problem of the model or the models which organize experience itself. Freud started off from a scientific horizon in which mechanicism and research on "forces" of a physicochemical order largely predominated in explaining all kinds of reality. In theorizing his own procedure, he had largely taken advantage of these preconditions, and not in a solely metaphorical fashion. The so-called economic and energetic side of his construction—an aspect based on the hypothesis of a "quantity" of excitation which can be variably displaced within the psychic apparatus—is a direct confirmation of this foundation. But what strikes one in Freud is, rather, the simultaneous presence of different models (energetic, dynamic-conflictual, topical), however heterogeneous to each other, which are positioned to give an account of the complex unity of analytic experience, avoiding the attempt to discard important elements that are irreducible to one or other of these models.

It was inevitable, however, that in the course of its diffusion the psychoanalytic discovery—insofar as it is centered on the relationship of man with himself, of consciousness with itself, and with the other of itself—encountered doctrines and disciplines that have always traditionally dealt with these problems. One can reasonably assert that this encounter—a collision and, also, a collusion—was perhaps the most significant element in the history of psychoanalysis in the last decades, and a not insignificant part of the history of Western culture.

To enter in a detailed fashion into this especially complex issue is impossible here. But one can identify the lines of a trend that, especially in the first half of the century, explicitly or implicitly underlies a large part of the "cultural" attempts at comprehending psychoanalysis and explaining it to itself, inserting it at the same time into the already understood. This trend consists of the attempt to reorient psychoanalysis to something external to it; at the extreme limit, it is translated into a systematic application of the reductive "nothing other than . . ." principle ("psychoanalysis is nothing other than . . ."), through which psychoanalysis is returned to the ambit of general psychology, of religion, of literature, of philosophy, of ethics, and so on, in even the most subtle and sophisticated of ways, and often at the hands of psychoanalysts themselves (Carl Gustav Jung, for example, can be considered the first great transcriber of the Freudian discovery in terms of a mythologizing spiritualism).

Next to these attempts, tendencies exist that are oriented toward "purifying" barbaric psychoanalysis, supplying it with patents of correct and generally acceptable scientificness, mostly modeled on the current state of the sciences (and thus, the substitution of models of a cognitivist, cybernetic, mathematical, or other type, for those "antiquated" ones used by Freud).

In recent years this kind of "capturing" of psychoanalysis has been declining, while the attempt to formalize psychoanalysis from the inside has been stronger, in an attempt to find the axis of its specific scientificness in its own mode of proceeding. Jacques Lacan's research on language is moving in this direction; beyond the lapidary formulae and his at once esoteric and exoteric performance, it represents one of the most interesting moments of this excavatory work within the analytic situation itself. This work is also being conducted in other directions, all based on the characteristics specific to the analytic relation, on the subversion of the spatiotemporal categories manifested in it, and so on.

These attempts at internal formalization have succeeded at least in part in overturning the already-mentioned tendency to assimilate psychoanalysis into traditional disciplines, giving way to an opposite course, that is to say, to an (imperialist? . . .) occupation of independent disciplines by psychoanalysis or by concepts derived from it.

5

We might admit that, continuing to work on its own terrain, psychoanalysis will succeed in elaborating its own autonomous scientific status, detaching itself from the innumerable interpretations which have saturated it in the course of the century. We might, however, also admit that, simultaneously, it will progressively reveal its own limit, which up to now has remained concealed by the overabundance of cultural constructions which took it as an object, in both positive and negative senses. It is an anthropological limit that will, in short, be discovered in the moment when, as we presume will happen, the current saturation of the cultural world by psychoanalysis will recede and it will appear to us more clearly defined as a historical-cultural "form." Let us try briefly to clarify this point.

The entire Freudian world, we have seen, is created through the incessant contact with human situations characterized by an inhibition, a block, a loss of vitality. Freud was well aware of this, so much so that he began to speak of *minderwertig* situations, which is to say, situations of lower quality, poor. Now, also characteristic of Freud is what we could call a movement of nostalgia for the world of human abundance, marked for him initially by the presence of art. From the point of view of his daily work and of the theory accompanying it, however, this world proves difficult to reach, if not unreachable. The theoretical difficulty presented by his concept of sublimation proves this directly. In his work on Leonardo da Vinci, Freud is relentless in the search for the passages, moments of resolution, and sudden turns which led the man from an orphaned childhood to the grandeur of the adult artist.

After Freud, in the triumphal success of psychoanalysis, the sense of blocked, impoverished situations, in which Freud and other psychoanalysts intervened, has progressively been lost. The hysteric, the Wolf Man, and Judge Schreber have become heroes of a cultural turn which has erased the traces of their own real difficulties. They have become true and proper heroes—not, as one sometimes hears, protagonists of psychoanalytic tales or novels, but genuine prototypical figures, in the same sense in which one can speak of Leonardo as having been among the greatest representatives of the myth of the artist. Emblematic figures of the splitting of the classical Subject—so they appear in Freud's description—have later acquired in culture a paradoxical, phantasmatic fullness.

How could this happen—how could an entire culture identify itself, through Freud's work, with these figures? We must suppose that something characteristic of Freud acts upon or acted within this culture, that is, the conception of a basic continuity of the psychic, which ignores the discontinuous and the radically different, differences between levels, and the leap or rupture which these imply. In Freud, this situation is explicitly confessed in the problematic and, in fact, nostalgic approach to the full, mythologized figures of the Renaissance. In the culture following in his wake, this nostalgia was lost, overwhelmed by the interest that his method aroused. The Freudian problem of (1) "*how one can become*" an artist à la Leonardo or a writer à la Dostoyevsky, surpassing the limits of the unconscious, has been lost and even in some cases, at least according to the common approach, has become the simple premise of (2) "*how one is*" an artist or writer from the outset, without posing the problem of the creative spark or leap which brings one to the work. In this sense, in his hesitations, Freud anticipates an epoch in which aesthetic experience disappears as a distinct, unified experience, and only comes to light or flashes up here and there, in contexts otherwise very different.

What is true of aesthetic experience could be repeated on other levels of the human, at first on an immediately contiguous level to the aesthetic one, which we could call the *ecstatic* level. This level is certainly, in our culture, at the boundaries of the taboo and the unsayable.

Today we detect signs of change precisely in these directions: the untouchable or the unsayable begins perhaps to make itself, little by little, practiced and practicable. It is at this point, we believe, that the anthropological and historical limit of Freudian psychoanalysis will become increasingly clear.

Freud's Chatter
Became a Tale

I'm assessing and weighing up a large tome that has just been published with the assistance of the Ministry of Public Education: *Psicoanalisi, arte e letteratura: Bibliografia generale 1900–1983* [Psychoanalysis, art and literature: a general bibliography 1900–1983] by Stefano Ferrari (Parma: Editrice Pratiche, 1985). An incredibly vast repertoire, containing almost seven thousand entries and accompanied by meticulous indexes: names, works, themes . . . in short, it is an exceptional tool and essential for anyone wishing to venture into the petrified forests where psychoanalysis runs alongside literature, firstly, but also art, cinema, criticism, etcetera. I can imagine the years of zeal and wasting away elapsed in libraries—and what libraries!—wearing out uncomfortable chairs and one's youth; I can intuit the crises, the doubts, perhaps also the confusion in the act of discovering, as was described in the introduction, that after 1967–1968, "there has been practically no critic, theoretician, or historian of art or literature who, in newspapers, journals, or periodicals of different culture and humanity, has not dedicated space, to a more or less relevant and more or less explicit degree, to the theme of the relations between art and psychoanalysis. In addition to the traditional and still prolific thread of applied psychoanalysis, which continues to fill the pages of psychoanalytic journals (moreover increasingly numerous), there is now a truly unverifiable mass of other studies and interventions." Thanks might be given to the well-regarded scholar who passed through this "unverifiable mass" and survived, and together with him, thanks might be given to the small publishing house which dared to publish the voluminous register.

In conclusion, a triumph? The testimony of an agreement made between psychoanalysis and art or literature, by now consolidated and peaceful? It would seem so, above all if one keeps in mind, after the first "applications" of psychoanalysis, the recent sophisticated orchestrations by critics and literati, who in these last years have read Freud, Jung, and especially Lacan passionately. Yet, on this immense production, by now diligently collected, a tenacious and often rather generic reserve seems always to have weighed, motionless. It is a kind of rumbling, a voice from below that continues to see in psychoanalysis a foreign, intrusive body and which can also be grasped, by contrast, in the demonstrative persistence of some of the scholars most involved in this agreement. Thus, the reader often has the impression of research that, increasingly elaborate and apparently exhaustive, is aimed at an ever-elusive object. Now, starting from within the psychoanalytic experience, I would like to try to clarify the meaning of this reserve, orienting myself through a point of view that does not seem to have emerged yet.

Analysis, strictly speaking, can be seen as a curious conversation in stages, in which the speaker—but also the listener—does not know (or *should not know*) where the conversation is going to end. In this situation of "double blindness," a specific relationship between two interlocutors is delineated, through unexpected fragments, either verbal or nonverbal, which is always singular and radically different in relation to what could be assumed by both the established knowledge of the analyst and the anxious questioning of the analysand. This relationship condenses in itself, at every instant, the past, present (*and future* . . . up to a certain point) of personal occurrences variously layered and grafted together, which emerge with a blind force, almost groping. At the same time, these can seem evanescent, because they are born from a *pratique du bavardage*, as Lacan says, which is to say chatter—but how unusual!—at variable intervals and with deferred responses, by syncopation, without a real dialogue. Ultimately, the essence of analysis is here, in this curious apparatus, and it passes through the words and silences exchanged between two interlocutors.

At this point, a fundamental problem arises when it comes to giving an external account of an experience which is irreducible to all other types of dialogue or meeting hitherto contrived by men. Freud was the first to find himself faced with this difficulty, and with various fluctuations in approach opted for a narrative form of communication to some extent, which implied omissions, displacements, entanglements, and so on (this aspect of Freud's writing has been examined very precisely by Mario Lavagetto in his recent *Freud, la letteratura e altro* [Freud, literature and more] (Turin: Einaudi, 1985).

The implicit basis of Freud's operation was of course that it was possible to pass easily between the experience of the spoken word and the written word; that in this passage there were merely problems of expressive conversion and that the best way to resolve these was to be found in the literary tradition to which he adhered. Consequently, the singular chatter of psychoanalytic treatment became, in Freud's writing, to his partial surprise, almost tales, narrative nuclei now more, now less elaborate. In this way, however, the analytic experience, predominantly *oral*, was received as the equivalent of a *written* text and as the ensemble of valid rules for the interpretation of written texts. This is confirmed by the frequent abuse, in recent years, of the term "text," or the nearby one of "tale," for almost any manifestation of analytic discourse. It is here that the implicit justification for any subsequent analysis of literary texts and works of art is rooted.

The first to turn in this direction was obviously Freud, and it is worth considering the reason behind the clear gap that can be seen between the disturbing grandeur of the real "clinical cases" (in particular "The Rat Man" and "The Wolf Man") and the flatness which at times insinuates itself into the most famous writings of "applied" psychoanalysis, for example his essays on Leonardo da Vinci and the *Moses* of Michelangelo. Given what I have just said, it is not difficult to identify the reason. In the former, there remain abundant traces of the richness, of the rush, of the *sudden* which runs through the analytic dialogue. What speaks to us still today is precisely the disaggregation of different materials, their accumulation and chasing one another around new poles. In the latter, notions and definitions that emerge there, in those singular aggregates, are approximated to situations that are certainly related to those which arise in analysis, with common roots, but where the reordering effect of writing and aesthetic selection have intervened profoundly. We are therefore faced with different, nonhomologous planes—hence the sense of inanity which takes hold of us when faced with certain operational behaviors. To take a basic example: one can pursue in analysis every vicissitude of the so-called Oedipus complex, and here the Sophoclean tragedy has been an illuminating aid. The inverse is not true: the analysis of the character of Oedipus in *Oedipus Rex* is an artificial addition. A similar difficulty also arises in the most recent and detailed analyses of formal structures: a linguistic equivalence is always presupposed between situations which are not equivalent. To conclude: analysis proper is enriched, in Freud and after Freud, by surprises and accidents in the twists and turns of the conversation. The analysis of texts and works, whatever the level of intelligence or subtlety lavished on these, is constrained to remain in line at the check-out desk of the psychoanalytic *library*.

If I permit myself such a direct tone, it is because the cultural passage from the spoken to the written word no longer seems natural and exclusive with the introduction of electronic means of communication; its scope seems limited. At the same time, the peculiarities of the spoken word, up until now "preyed upon" culturally by the written word, come forth into the clear light. In Freud's work, as in that of the *psychanalysant* literati who followed him, the privilege accorded to the written word is unreflective, almost absolute. Yet, while in Freud this privilege falls apart in the work of analysis, in the latter this is perpetuated in the most refined manners of the literary tradition. This also explains the weak reception of those who make this privilege the object of historical and anthropological research (among these,

I will mention Walter J. Ong, *Orality and Literacy: The Technologizing of the Word* [London: Methuen, 1982]).

Precisely this consciousness of what is radically new and different in the analytic experience—and which in certain ways is also archaic—could give meaning and fruitfulness to the wide array of studies involving psychoanalysis and art or literature. But it would do so on the condition of a true overturning of the object of examination. Analysis would no longer (or not only . . .) be disseminated into the boundless territories of literature, art, and various "humanities," but rather give rise to curiosity, rhetorical scrutiny, and scientific interest in a mode of investigative dialogue which is probably the most significant innovation introduced into Western discourse after the "noble sophistry" of Protagoras and Socrates.

Freud, Rilke, and Transience

A summer's day of 1913. In the blooming countryside, Sigmund Freud walks while conversing with a "taciturn friend" and a "young but already famous poet." The poet is struck by the beauty of the landscape, but at the same time appears profoundly saddened by the thought that all of this beauty, as also all human creation and beauty, is destined to disappear.

This is the beginning of a short text by Freud titled "On Transience," from two years after that conversation (1915).[85] Immediately one asks oneself: who is this "young but already famous poet" and who the "taciturn friend"? While the latter is characterized exclusively by his silence, which lasts throughout the whole conversation, the former is described very precisely. One might say that Freud intends to conceal the friend of silence completely, but the poet only partially—almost as though he wished to reveal him, while simultaneously not allowing him to be identified with certainty. Such a stroke of discretion-indiscretion is not infrequent in Freud.

In the Italian edition of Freud's *Works*, the editor Musatti, following the English *Standard Edition*, argues that it is unknown who these two interlocutors were.

However, on the basis of various indications, the hypothesis was put forward, some years ago now, that the young poet was Rainer Maria Rilke and the silent friend Lou Andreas-Salomé.[86] It is a hypothesis given credit by one of Freud's biographers and a personal friend, Max Schur. It is now time to examine its salient points.

In September 1913, during the psychoanalytic congress in Munich which marked the definitive break with Jung, Lou Salomé introduced Freud to the poet Rilke, who was thirty-seven years old. As we know, Lou, a rather well-known writer and an intimate friend of Nietzsche, had an intense relationship with Rilke and had for some years entered into the circles of those closest to Freud.

According to her account, Freud and Rilke began a long conversation, which lasted into the night. The hypothesis that sees the figure of Rilke in the "young poet" thus presupposes that the encounter and the conversation occurred on the margins of a congress, and not during a stroll in the countryside, some weeks before. Freud would have allowed himself in writing—as, after all, happened often—a sort of poetic license. He would have wanted to render the argument of the conversation—transience—live and immediate for the reader, placing it by contrast into the full splendor of nature in summer. In this manner, let me add, he would have succeeded in shifting the encounter away from the psychoanalytic scene, further rendering the two interlocutors unrecognizable. Transforming the female friend into a male friend, he would have been able to avoid creating the impression in the reader of a famous couple, which Rilke and Lou were.

Certainly, all of this does not at all confirm the hypothesis. The strongest point sustaining it is that the problem of transience vividly touched both Freud and Rilke in that period.[87] For Freud, the already foreseen rupture with Jung also implied, even more than the disappointment of the great hopes placed in the Swiss *goy*, whom he had considered until that point like a son and heir, the sense of a threat to the survival of psychoanalysis itself. On Rilke's part too, after the publication in 1910 of the *Notebooks of Malte Laurids Brigge* (a book intended as an "indescribable caesura" and "high watershed" moment), there had been a fall into a state of "weariness, a kind of aridity." For weeks or even months, he only just succeeded in putting together five lines of a letter. In this condition, feeling himself "one for whom nothing springs," the idea of undergoing analysis surged up. But this seemed to Rilke "too basic a help for me," which "helps once and for all, it tidies up." To find oneself "tidied up one day would perhaps be even more hopeless than this disorder." On the other hand, disturbances persisted in him, physically concentrated on his musculature, which he could no longer bear: "Certain bad habits, which I formerly always used to reach through as through stale air, are solidifying more and more, and I can conceive of their shutting me in someday like walls." It was thus necessary to find "a solution." Instead of turning directly to Freud, whose ideas on certain points made his "hair stand on end," a friend came in—Viktor Emil von Gebsattel, who later became a noted exponent of phenomenological psychiatry, and who gave Rilke the guarantee that he would use Freudianism "prudently and efficiently."

Here suddenly, like a miracle, was an interruption in his creative sterility. In January 1912 Rilke "receives" the first of the *Duino Elegies* and tells Lou of it in a "cry of exultation." Shortly afterward he also composes the second. Certainly, this is not enough to resolve the comprehensive state of inhibition, which will last around a decade; but it is enough to put the prospect of analysis into the background. Notably, both of the elegies have as their central theme the desperate consciousness of our transience and precariousness, counterposed to the essential consistency of the angels: "For we, even as we feel, evaporate in the act / of breathing ourselves out and beyond, / ember after ember, we burn away to nothing. / We give off an ever-diminishing scent."[88] Human life reveals its extreme and essential limits in some of the poet's identifications: abandoned lovers such as Gaspara Stampa, who is incorporated into "exhausted nature," and indistinct figures of "dead youths": "It's true enough, of course, no longer to live / on earth is strange, to abandon customs / barely mastered yet, not to interpret roses / and other auspicious things, not give them meaning / in a human future."[89]

It is a fading world, whose anguish is also manifested in the moment when an angel appears, since "jeder Engel ist schrecklich" (Every angel is terrifying).[90] In a note from Rilke to Lou from 1913, some months before the meeting with Freud, we find something which seems again to reprise, to the letter, in a more articulated fashion, the words of the unknown poet cited by Freud: "But when he approached the almond tree in blossom, he was startled nevertheless to find it so completely yonder, wholly gone over, wholly occupied there, wholly away from him."

Let us return now to Freud's short essay. Faced with the sadness of the young poet, Freud is pushed to retort: the transience of men and of nature does not debase them. On the contrary, it increases their value, which becomes the value of rarity: the beauty of nature returns, after being destroyed in winter, and this periodic return can be considered, in relation to the duration of our lives, an eternal return; as for the beauty of the work of art or the perfection of intellectual creation, these are valued only by our living consciousness and need not survive it. Yet, Freud adds, "I noticed that I had made no impression either upon the poet or upon my friend." (And nor on us, to tell the truth.) Freud questions the reason for this indifference and finds it in the fact that the poet *foresees* the end of what he looks upon and, together with it, the mourning he will face. It is the refusal of this mourning which stops him from enjoying the beauty which he has before him.

At this point, Freud abandons the description of the conversation and turns to current events, to the year 1915, which sees generalized destruction on an unheard-of scale occurring in Europe. All that was considered solid, durable, guaranteed, is revealed to be miserably transient. But even under these conditions, concludes Freud, when we will have overcome the mourning for the loss of what we have loved, "We shall build up again all that war has destroyed, and perhaps on firmer ground and more lastingly than before."

Even in this fearful world, Freud seems to say, I know that my position against the poet's view is right. All the commentators, as far as I know, have accepted Freud's conclusion without question. It corresponds to a *firm hope*, founded on the capacity to work through mourning following loss, even if this loss is immense.

If, however, we look more closely, things become complicated. The solid and durable world which Freud hoped would arise from catastrophe did not arise at all. On the contrary. In Europe there arose Nazism and Fascism, and with these there erupted a war even more dreadful than the first. Freud himself, through the construction of the death drive theory, came to doubt the possibility of opposing the generalized destruction. In a certainly different way, he arrived at a vision rather close to that of the young poet encountered years before. One might even think, quite unprompted, that the poet's voice, which Freud refused so certainly, corresponded to a secret voice inside him—but a voice that would emerge only *later*.

Later. This temporal dislocation brings us to reflect on the position of the poet. He does not rebel against a future mourning, as Freud claims, a little hastily, in his brief essay. Rather, the destruction is *already present* within him, at the moment when he contemplates that flowering countryside; mourning is already in him and it is a mourning that is irresolvable, since all things that live move toward their end, dying before one's eyes. These things are unique, *without substitute*, like the man who looks on ("Just *once* for each thing. *Once* and no more. / And we too, just *once* . . .").[91] Good common sense would hurry to remind him: you are beginning to mourn *before* the death of what you love. But the poet could respond, both to the men of good sense and to Freud in "On Transience": When you will all commence the work of mourning, destruction will have already taken place and your mourning will come *too late*; it will end up being only an attempt to move through a loss so enormous as to no longer be reparable. My mourning is foolish—and prescient; yours is wise—while simultaneously being belated, useless. At this point, the late Freud, the so-called pessimistic Freud of *Beyond the Pleasure Principle*, would perhaps agree with him.

So we have reached the most difficult and topical crux which underlies "On Transience." In the face of decay—and doesn't the word "decay" [*degrado*] imply a sort of stability and acceptance of *degradation* [*degradazione*]?—in the face of the advancing destruction of our "nature," which is after all the totality of our world, the easiest and thus far most frequent compensatory attitude is thinking that every object or situation is, after all, substitutable. Having overcome the mourning for the losses which we undergo each day, we set out leaping toward a new world, populated by ever-new substitutes. This attitude has clearly become insufficient, if not directly culpable. It corresponds to the position taken by the character of Freud, as staged in "On Transience": certainly not to that secret voice which will emerge later.

Must we agree with the young poet? Is it necessary to arrive at an anticipatory and mournful consciousness of the world? Do we have to make our voice into Cassandra's, foretelling the fall of the city and the extermination of the race? One cannot silence the sensation that any response given to *these* questions, which are moreover impending questions, risks being inert, irrelevant, completely generic.

But let us return to Rilke. Not, however, to the young melancholic poet of 1913, but rather to the Rilke of a decade later, who has passed through the period of the *Dürre*, of creative sterility, through the *Leidland*, the land of sorrows, without having been overcome by these, and has arrived in the last *Elegies* at a position where all that is native to this world, and as such radically ephemeral, seems to need us humans, "the most fleeting" of all, and it "call[s] to us strangely"; all things which "live while dying" believe us capable of saving them.[92]

This is the radical overturning of the ancient and commonplace position in which nature, the divine mother, was called to save us. Now it is *we* who are solicited to save her. In Rainer Maria Rilke, this overturning, reached by passing through the most painful identification with the ephemeral, shows up as the particular task of art and poetry (*to say* the Earth, to make it become *invisible*), which is at the same time an ethical-religious posture. Both presuppose something broader and more indistinct: the full acceptance of a figure which includes in itself and redeems earthly creatures before it is *too late*; a "heart," to use the words of the poet, in which there wells up the "Being, in abundance."[93] Perhaps one of the keys lies here, for us too, today. Perhaps it is not a work of mourning that we need, as Freud believed, neither anticipated nor *post rem*, but instead this welcoming, this capacity for empathy, in which we, wounded, will become the mother of wounded creatures. This is a difficult step; at the limit, impossible: *too late*. Yet it comes to us from all sides, and is increasingly often "solicited." In this task, a frail kind of happiness might be found; not an "*ascent*," an apex or climax as is often thought, but rather, as the *Tenth Elegy* tells us, a "*fall*," similar to the "rain falling on the dark earth in spring."[94]

The Emperor's Gift

Leafing through the pages Freud devoted, over the years, to the analysis of the "poor," I notice a curious repetition, almost a tic: every time he talks about the subject, he emphasizes his own difficulty or the impossibility of solving the problem and declares that, for the poor, *a therapy of the kind used by Joseph II*, the great Austrian emperor and successor of Maria Theresa, would be required.

This happens *three* times, in writings between 1913 and 1918. To summarize briefly: The poor person is able to detach from his neurosis only with great difficulty, since this neurosis allows him to reclaim as pity what men have denied him in terms of his material need, absolving him of the obligation to fight his poverty through work. Therefore, what is asked of the psychotherapist is in truth "a practical therapy of a very different kind— the kind which, according to our local tradition, used to be dispensed by the Emperor Joseph II."[95] Situations of real impasse, such as poverty, misfortune, unfortunate marital choice, and so on, would require "a very effective therapy . . . it would have to be of the kind which Viennese folklore attributes to the Emperor Joseph."[96] It is possible to predict that, in the future, the conscience of society will awaken and remind men that the poor person has a right to psychological assistance, like any other medical assistance; then new institutions will arise, in which a result may only be achieved by combining mental assistance with some form of material support, "in the manner of the Emperor Joseph."[97]

It is almost useless to point out the change undergone by the figure of the poor person in these writings, in the space of five years—running through, let us remember in passing, the First World War and the outbreak of the Russian Revolution. At the beginning, a negative tone is predominant, if not notes of condemnation, reflecting nineteenth-century attitudes. At the end, the poor person appears as a person who, in the future, will probably have the right to psychological assistance. In five years, one might say, the poor person goes from deserving to be sent to debtors' prisons, of which Dickens wrote, to being a client eligible for social assistance.

In any case, the reference to Joseph II's therapy remains constant. Freud does not have in mind, when he refers to him in these writings, the enlightened despot who introduced reforms that profoundly changed the structure of the state in the short space of ten years (1780–1790). Rather, he refers to the popular echo of this incisive government action, which reverberates in anecdotes and citations that spread out in an enduring manner. For example, the story of the widow who, harassed by a debt collector, is delivered a letter in which the debt is forgiven and the debt collector is dismissed. Here Joseph II is only the benefactor, the man "whose unconventional methods of distributing charity were notorious," according to a brief editorial note which appears in the *Standard Edition*.[98]

At this point we could conclude that the reference to the emperor in Freud is the repetition of an imperial-royal cliché, which does not imply any personal participation. But a curious annotation, next to one of the quotations just referred to, leaves us perplexed. Speaking of free treatments, that is, treatments that go beyond the usual monetary relationship and are conceived as a *gift*, a *favor*, Freud writes that, in the young man, neurotic resistance is found enormously increased by opposition to the obligation of gratitude, deriving from the paternal complex.[99] *Obligation and gratitude*: in the generality of the observation, there is something unexpected and singular.

In fact, the emperor Joseph II appears in one of the central dreams recounted in *The Interpretation of Dreams*, the dream titled "NON VIXIT," in which Freud discovers the basic ambivalence of his emotional life: the need to have both "an intimate friend and a hated enemy," which often coincide in the same person.[100] It is a dream experienced under the sign of *guilt*, precisely toward some of his friends. Entering the scene first is Ernst Fleischl, who had helped Freud financially and who died also because of Freud (who had recommended cocaine in order to free Fleischl from morphine). Then appear Wilhelm Fliess, his Berlin alter ego, and Joseph Paneth, another friend and benefactor who died prematurely. Fliess accuses Freud of indiscretion, for revealing his secrets to Paneth. Freud, "struck by strange emotions," says to Fliess: "non vixit," meaning to say that Paneth is dead and therefore doesn't know any of it. Then he looks with a penetrating gaze at Paneth, who becomes pale and dissolves. Freud is extraordinarily happy with this: he understands that Fleischl too, like Paneth, is only an apparition, a *revenant*, a person who exists and can be eliminated when desired.

In his dream, Freud later understands a current sense of guilt in his relations with his friend Fliess, living but at that moment ill, and further toward another friend, "who may be referred to by the name of Joseph"—Joseph Breuer, the great protector and benefactor of his youth. It is the second Joseph whom we meet in the marginalia of the dream. The connection to him is not remote, as it would seem at first sight. From a letter to Fliess we know that Freud, a few months earlier, had wanted to start repaying Breuer, but Breuer had refused, declaring that he considered the money he had given to Freud a *gift*.[101] This makes Freud literally furious and he vents to Fliess, accusing Breuer of "disdainful condescension" and an "unabated need to do good." "It is enough to make one extremely ungrateful for good deeds."[102]

In brief, Freud's position of guilt emerges, in which the indiscretion at the forefront in the dream is connected to another, more obscure, more ambiguous fault, which concerns *the acceptance or not of what is given by an authority*. In this case, what is at stake is the intellectual and economic help received from friends with authority. A dilemma arises: with these friends, does Freud have debts to pay, or has he received gifts for which he instead owes gratitude? The second option within this alternative is unacceptable to Freud. But if it is a question of debts, then these are *inexpungeable*, because the presumed creditor does not position himself as such but as a rescuer, friend, benefactor, and thus becomes a figure with whom one can never close accounts with a simple payment. The gift is a burden for Freud because he is unable to experience gratitude; but ingratitude is a fault, to which others can easily be adduced. In this light, the indiscretion of the dream is in giving something to someone, but something that is not ours, of which we only have the custody. It is a manner that *imitates* the behavior of authority and its mode of giving, but is stealthy, illicit, and therefore guilty.[103]

How does Freud try to get out of this situation? This is where the third Joseph of the dream appears, and it is precisely the emperor. Freud replies to Fliess, who accuses him, that Paneth "NON VIXIT," and annihilates

Paneth with his gaze. While the annihilating gaze refers to Professor Brücke, who had once reproached the
young Freud, the "NON VIXIT" refers to the base of the
statue of Joseph II, in the Hofburg in Vienna, on which
is written:

SALUTI PUBLICAE VIXIT
NON DIU SED TOTUS

(For the public well-being he lived not long but wholly.)
In Freud's memory, "PUBLICAE" is replaced by "PATRIAE"
or "fatherland" (and one of his biographers, Wittels,
has made various conjectures about this, accepted by
Freud).[104] But the most significant thing is the reversal
operated by the dream, from VIXIT NON DIU to NON VIXIT,
posing thus the *non* as a term valid for the preceding
word instead of for the following, almost as in the famous oracle which Freud perhaps knew: IBIS REDIBIS
NON MORIERIS IN BELLO (You will go, you will come back,
you will not die in war). The grammatical reversal entails
a reversal of the action of the monarch: the beneficent
action (in favor of the *salus publica*) becomes an action
in which absolute power over life and death comes to
the fore. In fact, Freud, using a part of the inscription,
we could say a fragment of imperial language, "exercises justice," as he himself declares, and pronounces
a verdict of death—NON VIVIT [he is not living]—which
as soon as it is mitigated, or further displaced, returns

to being NON VIXIT [he did not live], and concerns all the other friend-protectors toward whom the dreamer feels at fault.

Added to this, Freud signals an ambivalent relationship with a nephew, older than him by a year, with whom as a boy he had recited an act from the tragedy *The Robbers* by Schiller, playing Brutus, the nephew of Caesar. Now, in a footnote, Freud detects that Caesar refers to the *Kaiser*, the emperor, and thus again to Joseph II.

At this point, however, one cannot suppress the impression that Freud stays away from this figure. He insists on his private, current relationships or those of the distant past, but avoids confronting himself directly with the looming shadow to which his friends, elder nephew, or younger brother—named *Julius*, though not named here[105]—are connected by some significant traits. These figures can even be considered representatives of this shadow, but are absolutely minuscule compared to the imperial presence. It is this presence, as the supreme regulating power over life and death, which is central in the dream. Freud catches a glimpse of it, we could say, when he dissolves his friend using a fragment of the phrase written on the base of the statue—standing thus *at the foot* of the statue. This fragment is presented like a *formula*, and after having pronounced it, the dreamer, with recourse to the annihilating gaze of his old professor, can make his friend disappear. It is therefore a *magical* dissolution, and is certainly not an effective solution for his guilt, as it may have seemed to some commentators. He imitates an aspect of the supreme power and magically becomes extremely powerful; in reality, as we have seen, he continues to feel guilty.

Now, it is important to note that the imperial authority is linked to the authority of Professor Brücke, but is also clearly distinct from it and transcends it absolutely. It is from this imperial authority that the power of the professor derives, borrowed here by Freud, but it remains on another level, which can be grasped only marginally. It is an axiomatic power, so to speak, independent of the figures of parental or other authority to which it is connected, a power that is resorted to, it would seem, at the moment when an intervention *in extremis*—magical, miraculous—is necessary. We are in a territory that can easily be defined as unreal, but not nonexistent; on an unconscious level that is different from the one populated by familiar figures, and which appears at the point when particularly difficult or unsolvable problems are at stake.[106]

We might catch ourselves fantasizing about what the development of Freud's research (and the whole of psychoanalysis) would have been if, instead of addressing only immediate representatives of power and authority—parents, relatives, friends, etcetera—the problem of this disturbing central instance of authority were posed, here embodied by Joseph II. Its appearance is a culmination of the dream but is not scrutinized or investigated; it remains on the margins of the interpretation, as if it were a detail secondary to the primary importance of familiar figures.

Only many years later did Freud turn directly and without mediation to look at this absolute condition, in which life and death, the beginning and the end, coincide, charging it with a dichotomous mythical image: Eros and Thanatos. He eventually encountered what in equally mythical but more incisive terms is presented for the single individual as *tyche*, chance, and which for all individuals, for all living beings, is *ananke*, necessity.

But for the time being, we must perhaps resign ourselves to *also* seeing in the NON VIXIT a magical formula which reassures Freud about the very nonexistence of this supreme power. In addition to Freud's friend-enemies, the NON VIXIT may also concern the very power of which he makes use. It is essentially grasped as a power of death; and if in waking life it is not possible to consider it nonexistent, we must beware of it, keep as far away from it as possible. It is legitimate to ask whether, faced with this dream, Freud's retreat, which is also a furtive imitation of what he withdraws from, does not also reverberate in corresponding attitudes and behaviors of his waking life.

In this regard, we might refer to the central relationship of Freud's life, that with Wilhelm Fliess, which was characterized by a collusive, secret alliance, opposed to an enemy world, between two people animated by the desire to *found* a new science. The same is true of the psychoanalytic institution, which, before meeting a bureaucratic fate, so evident today, was a semi-esoteric group, controlled in its decisive years (from 1912 until nearly 1927) by a secret "committee" of seven people, who exchanged cameos and rings as a pledge of loyalty to the Master, against secessionists and dissidents.[107] There is something childish here, something of the fairy tale, which borrows a fragment of magical power, precisely as Freud does in the dream.

These attitudes are the external, most visible part of the major difficulty in meeting the figure of supreme power: the relationship with its vital, free, and liberating aspect, synthesized as we have seen in the capacity to give gifts. Here Freud moves with considerable awkwardness, and his impasse is revealed in the reduction of the gift, and of the multiplicity of meanings that can be assumed at each turn, to a purely coercive, subordinating *obligation*. This is seen most clearly in the case of Breuer. One can certainly speculate on the personal reasons for this situation, which leads to the unresolvable guilt spoken of in the dream's "NON VIXIT." But, again, here we are interested in the public side of this setting. Freud's personal phobia of the gift was reflected in the psychoanalytic institution in the explicit refusal of individual gifts from patients, due to the total insertion of analytic treatment into the general exchange relationship. The prescription of this refusal was subsequently widely criticized and analyzed; much less so was the relationship to money, so precise, so mandatory, and so closely linked to time, to the (chronometric?) duration of the analytic work.

The money economy has left no room for the gift economy, one could say, and in this sense Freud's singular inhibition anticipated that general decline of the gift, on which contemporary criticism has focused.[108] Was this inevitable? Freud certainly saw no other way to go about his activities, as we do not, *usually*. But today we are paying for the automatism of this obligatory choice, and we no longer feel it as eternally valid. *Every historical moment, individual or collective, in which the money relationship, the mercenary relationship, reveals its limits and is exceeded, even fleetingly, is also a moment when the institutional analytic relationship enters into crisis.* This is the moment when the strongest and most general meaning of the problem of the analysis of the poor is revealed. In this moment of crisis, the poor paradoxically become the image of a human condition *beyond money*, *richer*, less restricted by the straitjacket of exchange. This condition involves requests for recognition and for love, with respect to which institutional analysis appears to be an inadequate surrogate and is therefore refused. This is the moment when the ingenious situation invented by Freud reveals its essential deficiency—quickly covered up, but which persists, immobile, incurable, invisible until the next crisis.

The Unexpected and Surprise in Analysis

I would like to make some observations, to pose some problematic, perhaps somewhat paradoxical, points. I begin with an episode which came to my mind when Marisa Fiumanò was speaking. One day Michael Balint, Ferenczi's student, receives a gentleman who asks to begin an analysis with him. This gentleman speaks at length and Balint doesn't understand what he's saying, what his problem is. He brings him back for another session and Balint still doesn't understand. At the end, he says to the gentleman: "Look, I really don't understand what you're saying to me," and the other says, "Exactly, this itself was the test I wanted you to undergo: to go to an analyst, recount untrue things to him and see if he notices. I went to other analysts, who told me various things, who gave me interpretations, and it's only you who noticed." Lacan notes that Balint's declaration is in the true sense the beginning of analysis. I completely agree, and I believe we all have the same impression. I propose thus to examine this particular analytic moment attentively. Clearly, Balint did not give an *interpretation*. Yet many maintain that giving an interpretation is the precipitating task, if not the sole task, of an analyst; and moreover, often, an explanatory interpretation, comprising all that has been said before. This conception of analysis, which is very common, has given rise to a tendency I would describe as *omniexplicability*, which is ruinously active both within analysis itself and outside of analysis, in the popular psychoanalytic jargon. Balint, we have seen, does something different: he says something that is both true and surprising for himself, he says that he doesn't understand, and it is precisely this not understanding which establishes contact. He thus makes an intervention which is properly analytical, which however is not absolutely an interpretation in the proper sense, but rather a wager, a move which ignores its own consequences. In fact, it could have happened that the gentleman thought: "But really! This analyst is stupid." Balint wasn't afraid of this consideration, probably he didn't even think of it, and the result—as unexpected for him as for the patient, who expected to find an "intelligent," "understanding" analyst to fool and then to leave—is the real beginning of analysis.

This distinction between analytic intervention and interpretation as *one* of the modalities of intervention seems important and applies to many other situations. David Meghnagi spoke to us of the multiplicity of things that can legitimately enter into analysis. Let me add: provided they enter at the *right moment*. Here, for example, the case of the *Witz*, the joke. Meghnagi told us that in essence psychoanalysis is the joke of a Jew against Western society. Now, this statement is itself a joke, and if it has struck us, or at least has struck me, it is because it came at the right moment, after several dense, profound, heavy reports . . . This joke gave me a sense of lightness, a thrust forward toward what Meghnagi would say following this and also, simply, the desire to repeat it, to keep it present. Now, even the joke, provided it comes at the right moment, can be a fertile analytic intervention. The same can be said for the *variable length* of the session, linked to the name of Lacan and presented as a surprising punctuation, making one pose questions and interrogations later. In late Lacan, this kind of interruption seems almost to have become the sole motor of analysis, with sessions of a few minutes: here I signal a privileging, which seems to me to be analogous to the way in which the majority of analysts privilege interpretation of a comprehensive type. In any case, there remains the illuminating value of the Lacanian *move*. The problem of the *gift* is also posed in the same way, which is so intensely refused theoretically by Freud, yet so present in concrete practice, as we know from various sources.

I could, of course, continue at length in this listing, but it's clear that the delicate point, which is undecidable *a priori*, is that of the *right moment*, the moment which articulates the situation and projects it toward the future. When one recounts an anecdote, it is told successfully if those who listen laugh; if they don't laugh, something isn't going right, either in the story itself, in the mode of telling it, or in the person listening. Success implies a sort of instantaneous recapitulation of what has been said in an unforeseen instant, joyous, light, which hastens toward other narrations, which pushes forward. This is what occurs in a successful analytic intervention, and what makes us feel that it has succeeded.

For me, the *surprise* element in analysis has become ever more significant over the course of the years. Surprising and letting oneself be surprised, in both interlocutors, seems necessary so that the analysis can proceed; or I would say, instead, so that there can be analysis *tout court*. Otherwise there is just a ministering and administering of knowledge, repetition of the already known, which finds its peak probably in so-called didactic analyses. In my opinion, nothing is active if it is not brought forward by and in surprise; and everything can be active and fecund (wordplay, joke, length of session, etcetera, and also, obviously, interpretation) if it is born as unexpected surprise. Naturally, this moment of surprise cannot be calculated; it bursts forth suddenly, interrupting the uniform flow of time. It is thus clear that it's not a matter of becoming professionals of surprise, people who at every moment draw a new rabbit out of a hat. If that were the case, we would fall back again into a repetitive situation, and there would be no more surprises but only conscious tricks, exhausted in their effect already at the outset. Further, our procedures would come dangerously close to suggestion, which certainly is present in every case, but which it is up to us to control and reduce.

At this point, the problem of the relationship between this setting and transference might be posed. Now, we no longer believe in transference as resistance in analysis, in the original Freudian sense. It appears to us instead as a ubiquitous element present in every relationship. But precisely because of this nonspecific, universal extension, it remains necessary to specify that transference is often a placeholder concept for us, something analysts use to indicate different states of any relationship each individual time, managing thereby to conceal the *truth* of the relationship itself. What I mean is that the notion of transference is often used in an all-encompassing way, so as to cover over, more than reveal, the concrete situation. This is due, in my opinion, to the fact that transference tends to be *inferred* mechanically, consciously, from events that have occurred in the past and from the events of treatment themselves. Otherwise it is inferred capriciously, case by case, according to the variations of the so-called countertransference of the analyst (an altogether infelicitous term, which should be replaced at least with "the analyst's transference"). The situation of transference is made explicit instead *a posteriori, nachträglich* [retroactively], equivalent to the analytic intervention of which I have spoken, and turns out to be completely independent of our conscious, preconstituted conceptions. Here Bion's advice is worth considering: "Without memory and without desire"—which does not mean proposing the figure of an oblivious and aseptic analyst, as we often hear spoken of; rather the necessity that the analyst suspend his memory and desire, letting thus emerge, through the analytic *epoché*, the new and the unexpected, in which transference is included.

This formulation of the analytic intervention and of transference can be tested, thinking back to our own analysis itself, or listening to someone speak of their past analysis. I believe that we seldom have, in memory, a series of closely woven interpretations; rather, together with some key turning-point interpretations, and some silences which are as meaningful, there come to mind loose details, curious moments that appear to be insignificant, movements in which are embodied what a friend of mine, Lamberto Boni, calls "an encounter." Something here does not correspond to the situation of transference as it is often understood; but rather it is something that approaches what the Greeks called good or bad fortune, *tyche*, which then oddly enough, by different routes, is connected to *ananke*, which is to say, the inevitability of the destiny of all of us.

Note on the Texts

The first publication dates and sources of the texts in this volume are given below.

"Freud" in *Il XIX secolo: la rivoluzione industriale* [The nineteenth century: The Industrial Revolution], vol. 11 in *I protagonisti della storia universale* [The protagonists of universal history] (Milan: Compagnia Edizioni Internazionali, 1966), 365–392.

"Psychoanalysis" ("Psicoanalisi") was written in 1984 for Garzanti's *Enciclopedia europea* [European encyclopedia], but was not published.

"Freud's Chatter Became a Tale" ("E le chiacchiere di Freud diventarono racconto") in *Corriere della Sera*, May 1, 1986.

"Freud, Rilke and Transience" ("Freud, Rilke e la caducità") in *il manifesto*, January 22–23, 1989.

"The Emperor's Gift" ("Il dono dell'imperatore") in *il manifesto*, April 2–3, 1989.

"The Unexpected and Surprise in Analysis" ("Imprevisto e sorpresa in analisi") in *Il tempo del transfert* [The time of transference], ed. Marisa Fiumanò (Milan: Guerini e Associati, 1989), 173–176.

[Translator's note: References to Freud's works have been presented as references to the *Standard Edition*.]

Notes

Introduction by Gioele P. Cima

1. Fachinelli's most important translations of Freud include those of "Negation" (1965); *The Interpretation of Dreams* (1966); *Leonardo da Vinci, A Memory of His Childhood* (1974); and several "Papers on Technique."

2. S. Vegetti Finzi, *Storia della psicoanalisi. Autori, opere, teorie 1895–1990* (Milan: Mondadori, 2017), 29. Unless otherwise noted, all translations in the introduction are by Gioele P. Cima (revised by Lorenzo Chiesa).

3. M. David, *La psicoanalisi nella cultura italiana* (Turin: Boringhieri, 1966), 569n.

4. Cesare Musatti (1897–1989) was a leading figure of the first generation of Italian psychoanalysts. He wrote a famous treatise on psychoanalysis. He was also the Italian editor of Freud's works and one of the main founders of the Società Psicoanalitica Italiana.

5. Besides Fachinelli, the group included the philosophers Luciano Amodio, Giancarlo Majorino, the scholar of German literature Giorgio Dolfini, and the historian Sergio Caprioglio.

6. E. Fachinelli, L. Muraro, and G. Sartori, eds., *L'erba voglio. Pratica non autoritaria nella scuola* (Turin: Einaudi, 1971).

7. See G. Contri, ed., *Lacan in Italia. 1953–1978* (Bellinzona: La Salamandra, 1978).

8. E. Fachinelli, *Il bambino dalle uova d'oro* (Milan: Adelphi, 2010).

9. See E. Fachinelli, *Uma tentativa de amor* (Rome: Cooperativa Scrittori, 1976).

10. See the English translation, E. Fachinelli, *The Still Arrow: Three Attempts to Annul Time*, trans. L. Chiesa (London: Seagull, 2021).

11. See D. Borso, "Fachinelli, Eco e l'eroina," in *Minima et Moralia* (1988), http://www.minimaetmoralia.it/wp/fachinelli-eco-leroina/.

12. E. Fachinelli, *Claustrofilia: Saggio sull'orologio telepatico in psicanalisi* (Milan: Adelphi, 1983).

13. E. Fachinelli, *La mente estatica* (Milan: Adelphi, 1989).

14. These include, in addition to work by Lea Melandri, texts by the psychoanalysts Sergio Benvenuto and Massimo Recalcati (the latter is the author of the first monograph on Fachinelli) and Dario Borso (who is scrupulously working on the Fachinelli Archive in Luserna and editing his posthumous writings in Italian).

15. See E. Fachinelli, "Cultura e necrofagia nell'industria culturale," in "Elvio Fachinelli. Un freudiano di giudizio," ed. A. Sciacchitano, special issue, *aut aut* 352 (2011): 21–26.

16. Fachinelli, *La mente estatica*, 16.

17. E. Fachinelli, "A proposito di Jung," in *Il bambino dalle uova d'oro*, 97.

18. See S. Benvenuto, "La 'gioia eccessiva' di Elvio Fachinelli," in *Intorno al '68. Un'antologia di testi*, ed. M. Conci and F. Marchioro (Rome: Massari Editore, 1998), 249–278.

19. See E. Glover, *Technique of Psychoanalysis* (New York: HarperCollins, 1955).

20. See H. Marcuse, *Eros and Civilization: A Philosophical Inquiry into Freud* (Boston: Beacon Press, 1992).

21. See E. Fachinelli, "Il contributo del test di Rorschach all'analisi strutturale della nevrosi fobico-ossessiva," *Rivista sperimentale di freniatria* 85 (1961): 1723–1787.

22. Ibid., 1721.

23. Ibid., 1725.

24. Ibid., 1726.

25. E. Fachinelli, "Nuovo significato del disegno magico e recupero del passato nell'opera di un'artista psicotica," in *Archivio di psicologia, neurologia e psichiatria* 25, no. 1 (1964): 27–50.

26. See G. Bonoldi, "Perché una ristampa?," in *Il Corpo. 1965–1968*, ed. G. Bonoldi (Milan: Moizzi Editore, 1976), ix–x.

27. E. Fachinelli, "L'ipotesi della distruzione in Sigmund Freud," in *Il bambino dalle uova d'oro*, 25–42.

28. Ibid., 37.

29. Ibid., 36.

30. Ibid., 27.

31. Ibid., 33.

32. E. Fachinelli, "Sul tempodenaro anale," in *Il bambino dalle uova d'oro*, 43–70.

33. Ibid., 46.

34. Ibid., 47.

35. Ibid., 68–69.

36. See N. Balestrini and P. Moroni, eds., *L'orda d'oro 1968–1977. La grande onda-ta rivoluzionaria e creativa, politica ed esistenziale* (Milan: Feltrinelli, 1997).

37. E. Fachinelli, "Il desiderio dissidente," in *Il bambino dalle uova d'oro*, 141–149.

38. Ibid., 149.

39. Ibid., 143.

40. Ibid., 147.

41. Ibid., 147–148.

42. E. Fachinelli, "Gruppo chiuso o gruppo aperto?," in *Il bambino dalle uova d'oro*, 150–183.

43. E. Fachinelli, "Il Sessantotto," in *Al cuore delle cose. Scritti politici (1967–1989)*, ed. D. Borso (Rome: DeriveApprodi, 2016), 39.

44. Fachinelli, "Gruppo chiuso o gruppo aperto?," 170.

45. M. Recalcati, *Critica della ragione psicoanalitica: Tre saggi su Elvio Fachinelli* (Milan: Ponte alle Grazie, 2020), 21.

46. See E. Fachinelli, "Che cosa chiede Edipo alla Sfinge?," in *Il bambino dalle uova d'oro*, 187–203.

47. Ibid., 190.

48. Ibid., 189.

49. Ibid., 197.

50. Ibid., 202.

51. E. Fachinelli, "Un testo cinese," in Borso, *Al cuore delle cose*, 24.

52. Ibid., 25.

53. E. Fachinelli, "Programma per un teatro proletario di bambini," in *Il bambino dalle uova d'oro*, 204–217.

54. Ibid., 211.

55. See E. Fachinelli, "Scassabambini," in *Il bambino dalle uova d'oro*, 228–234.

56. E. Fachinelli, "Lo psicoanalista deve definire la sua posizione in società," *aut aut* 15 (1970).

57. E. Fachinelli, "Il paradosso della ripetizione," in *Il bambino dalle uova d'oro*, 275–322.

58. Ibid., 310.

59. Ibid., 306–307.

60. See E. Fachinelli, "Replica di Elvio Fachinelli," in *Psicologi e società*, ed. F. Ceccarello and F. De Franceschi (Milan: Feltrinelli, 1974), 170.

61. Fachinelli, *The Still Arrow*, 5.

62. Ibid., 128.

63. Ibid., 5.

64. Ibid., 10.

65. Ibid., 12.

66. Ibid., 84.

67. Ibid., 95, 100.

68. Ibid., 52, 101.

69. Ibid., 50–51.

70. Fachinelli, *Claustrofilia*, 142.

71. Ibid., 64.

72. Ibid., 43.

73. Ibid., 51.

74. Fachinelli, *La mente estatica*, 12.

75. Ibid., 102.

76. Ibid., 76.

77. Ibid., 17.

78. Ibid., 20.

79. See F. Furedi, *Therapy Culture: Cultivating Vulnerability in an Uncertain Age* (New York: Routledge, 2003).

80. E. Fachinelli, "Il denaro dello psicoanalista," in *Sessualità e politica. Documenti* (Milan: Feltrinelli, 1976), 308.

81. Ibid., 314.

On Freud

82. S. Freud, "Die Struktur der Elemente des Nervensystems," *Jahrbücher für Psychiatrie und Neurologie* 5 (1884): 221–229.

83. S. Freud, *On Aphasia*, trans. E. Stengel (London: International Universities Press, 1953).

84. References to Exodus are from *Tanakh: A New Translation of the Holy Scriptures According to the Traditional Hebrew Text* (Philadelphia: Jewish Publication Society, 1985).

85. S. Freud, "On Transience" [*SE*, 14: 305–307].

86. For the hypothesis that the "silent friend" is Lou Salomé, see H. Lehmann in *The Psychoanalytic Quarterly* 35 (1966): 423–427.

87. For the biographical references to Rilke and quotations from him, see *Rainer Maria Rilke and Lou Andreas Salomé: The Correspondence*, ed. E. Pfeiffer (New York: Norton, 2006).

88. R. M. Rilke, *The Duino Elegies*, trans. M. Crucefix (London: Enitharmon, 2006), 23.

89. Ibid., 19.

90. Ibid., 15.

91. Ibid., 69.

92. Ibid.

93. Ibid., 73.

94. Ibid., 81.

95. S. Freud, "On Beginning the Treatment" (1913) [*SE*, 12: 133].

96. S. Freud, *Introductory Lectures on Psychoanalysis*, Lecture XXVII [*SE*, 16: 431].

97. S. Freud, "Lines of Advance in Psycho-Analytic Therapy" (1918) [*SE*, 17: 166].

98. Freud, *Introductory Lectures on Psychoanalysis*, 431. In another note, Freud mentions the Emperor Joseph II of Austria (1741–1790) "about whose unconventional methods of philanthropy many legends were current" [*SE*, 17: 166].

99. Freud, "On Beginning the Treatment," 132.

100. The dream is from 1898 and thus predates the three citations of the "benefactor" Joseph II by decades. Here we must remark that Freud worked for many years in the children's hospital founded by the emperor. There are not, as far as I know, other references to the latter in the works of Freud.

101. Cited in D. Anzieu, *Freud's Self-Analysis* (London: Hogarth Press and Institute of Psycho-Analysis, 1986), 381.

102. Sigmund Freud, letter to Wilhelm Fliess, January 16, 1898, in *The Complete Letters of Sigmund Freud to Wilhelm Fliess: 1887–1904* (Cambridge, MA: Belknap Press of Harvard University Press, 1985), 294–295.

103. Added to the fault of indiscretion is the fault of theft or plagiarism, which appears at the forefront in Freud's relationship with Fliess.

104. Cited in Anzieu, *Freud's Self-Analysis*, 380.

105. Ibid., 383.

106. These problems are posed, for example, in the psychoses (the dissolving enacted by Freud in the dream recalls a movement of maniacal exit from a depression). The "axiomatic power" here condensed might plausibly be related to the "hole" left by *Verwerfung*, the foreclosure of the name-of-the-father in Lacan—as its "positive" and *tremendous* equivalent—and to the schizophrenic "deterritorialized flows" of Deleuze and Guattari. But we can also think of normal or supernormal performances (for example, the adolescent poltergeist).

107. See E. Jones, *The Life and Work of Sigmund Freud*, vol. 2 (London: Hogarth Press, 1955).

108. See, for example, T. W. Adorno, *Minima Moralia* (London: Verso, 2005).